Praise for *Tarot, No Questions Asked*

"This delightful, unpretentious, straight-from-the-heart book by one of Tarot's great ambassadors to the world teaches us—all of us, from beginners to longtime professionals—how to become better readers." —Rachel Pollack, author of *Seventy-Eight Degrees of Wisdom*

"Theresa Reed has produced yet another invaluable resource for the modern Tarot reader. She makes you feel immediately at home through the fascinating stories and adds a lovely dash of fun to serious exercises. Even a seasoned reader will feel their work deepen through Theresa's careful tutelage. An absolute must for every Tarot reader's bookshelf." —Courtney Weber, author of *Tarot for One*

"Intuitive readings seem like something you should just be able to do, right? Intuition comes from within, after all. The problem comes when we start second-guessing ourselves. Theresa Reed takes you by the hand in her new book, *Tarot: No Questions Asked*. Every time you start to doubt yourself, Theresa will take your hand and lead you through the numbers, symbols, and meanings of these cards that have become her life. She will help you answer every question you have so that you can trust your intuition completely and use the cards with confidence. Everyone wants to learn from a master, right? Here's your chance." —Melissa Cynova, author of *Kitchen Table Magic, Kitchen Table Tarot,* and *Tarot Elements*

"Theresa Reed nails the essential beginner's quest to move from learning to actually reading for others. Her approachable point of view allows the reader to dive into each card in a very tangible way. I particularly like how she sprinkled her own personal experiences—good and bad—to create an authentic book on how to read the Tarot cards. She doesn't hold back in offering her knowledge which, with her many years as a professional reader, has the depth that so many other books lack. I would recommend this book to my own students as well as anyone looking to gain experiential practice with Tarot." —Arwen Lynch, the Professional Joy Seeker

"Theresa's mission is 'always to help and guide.' And she does that with true commitment and dedicated service to her readers, to assist them in becoming better helpers and guides themselves. She knows how to tell a compelling story and makes learning all about the Tarot fun, fascinating, and powerful, too." —Amy Zerner and Monte Farber, bestselling authors of *The Enchanted Tarot, Enchanted Love Tarot*, and *Instant Tarot*

"Theresa Reed once again goes above and beyond with *Tarot: No Questions Asked*. This book promises to walk us through reading Tarot when there's no specific question in mind, and it absolutely comes through on that promise. That alone would have been satisfying enough. Instead of leaving us satisfied though, Reed dives into helping us deepen our intuition with Tarot exercises that will be brand new to many readers and then tops it off with a section on how to take our Tarot skills to a professional level in a book that is as warm and friendly as it is informative. Reed leaves us feeling ecstatic and excited for our Tarot-filled lives and left me feeling eternally grateful for her presence and work in the worldwide Tarot community." —Cassandra Snow, author of *Queering the Tarot* and *Queering Your Craft*

"*Tarot: No Questions Asked* is an excellent representation of author Theresa Reed's work. It is written in a voice that is straightforward, down to earth, and that all levels of Tarot readers (or those wishing to learn to read the Tarot) will relate to.

"She brings the cards to life through stories and exercises (called Tarotcizes), showing the reader how to access the magic that the Tarot can be. Her aim is to educate the readers on the cards, connect readers to their intuitive self, and show them how to read the cards intuitively.

"The images in this book are from the classic Rider-Waite-Smith Tarot deck. Reed presents a solid foundation for the cards, then shows how they form a story during a reading. She discusses reversals, how cards can be read together, how to apply suits and numbers, and uses exercises termed 'Tarotcizes' to challenge readers and to expand their perspective of the cards.

"Reed also addresses the subject of going pro—what the pros and cons are and what the reader needs to pay attention to in order to set up their business properly.

"There is a strong sense of both ethics and responsibility in Reed's writing—something that is very important at all times. This is a book that you don't just read once and shelve—it is a resource that brings something new every time you use it!" —Bonnie Cehovet is a professional Tarot reader, author of *Tarot, Birth Cards and You; Tarot, Rituals, and You; Seek Joy… Toss Confetti; Invisible Me; Surviving the Holidays;* reviewer; and contributor to *The Cartomancer*

"*Tarot: No Questions Asked* summarizes Theresa Reed's philosophy on reading Tarot. Her no-nonsense, trust-your-gut approach to learning cards is easy to grasp and learn. Chock full of examples and exercises, Reed directs you to trust the stories contained in the cards and the little voices we all have to provide truthful and insightful answers. Interested in learning the art of the modern intuitive Tarot reading? Then don't pass this book up." —Jaymi Elford, author of *Tarot Inspired Life*

"Theresa Reed's *Tarot: No Questions Asked* is a fresh take on all things Tarot. Here the guiding principle is less a series of questions we ask the cards by rote and more an encouragement to take our experience of and relationship with the cards to a deeper, more intuitive level. It is an approach that yields so much wonderful insight, and Theresa's guidance is full of love and wisdom in equal measure. A wonderful and needed addition to anyone's magical library." —Briana Saussy author of *Making Magic*

"There is a reason that Theresa Reed is THE TAROT LADY: she is a Tarot fountain of knowledge. *Tarot: No Questions Asked* is a wonderful resource to get your intuitive Tarot readings to the next level. Perfect for beginners and people who already read the cards. This book is another fantastic resource by Theresa and I highly recommend it!" —Ethony Dawn, author of *Your Tarot Court*, and headmistress at *www.tarotreadersacademy.com*

"In *Tarot: No Questions Asked*, Theresa Reed shares her years of hands-on experience and her immense wisdom with the Tarot, intuition, and professional reading practices. With her usual wit and no-nonsense approach, Reed invites both novice and seasoned readers to *live* the Tarot, rather than just practice or memorize the meanings. Within the pages of this book you'll discover new and exciting ways to work with the Tarot in a fluid and intuitive style. For me, Tarot is an ever-evolving body of knowledge, rooted in personal empowerment and reflection. As a Tarot visionary, Reed passes on the sacred torch for the future of Tarot to continue. I know *Tarot: No Questions Asked* will become a classic text. If you are interested in expanding your intuition and deepening your practice with Tarot, if you want to cultivate success as a professional reader, then you need this book. This information is rarely shared with such depth and approachability."

—Shaheen Miro, author of *The Lunar Nomad Oracle* and *Lunar Alchemy*, and coauthor of *Tarot for Troubled Times*

TAROT

NO QUESTIONS ASKED

Mastering the Art of
Intuitive Reading

THERESA REED

FOREWORD BY RACHEL POLLACK

WEISER
BOOKS

Dedicated to my mother, Margaret Linder,
for teaching me to trust my gut.

This edition first published in 2020 by Weiser Books, an imprint of
Red Wheel/Weiser, LLC
With offices at:
65 Parker Street, Suite 7
Newburyport, MA 01950
www.redwheelweiser.com

ISBN: 978-1-57863-713-3
Library of Congress Cataloging-in-Publication Data available upon request.

Cover and text design by Kathryn Sky-Peck
Typeset in Warnock Pro

Printed in Canada
IBI
10 9 8 7 6 5 4

Contents

Living a Tarot Life

This delightful, unpretentious, straight-from-the-heart book by one of Tarot's great ambassadors to the world teaches us—all of us, from beginners to longtime professionals—how to become better readers. More skilled, more knowledgeable, more able to serve the people who come to us for readings. And yet, it is more than that. Teaching by example, Theresa shows us how to bring our whole lives to the practice of reading the cards. For really, there is no other way to do it.

I have been reading Tarot for over fifty years, and I can tell you two things for certain. One is that you will never come to the end of it. Because Tarot is not a book of fixed pages, or a set doctrine, but changes every time we shuffle the cards, it will always show us new things, new ideas, new discoveries. And because the impetus for shuffling the deck is a question—*Every reading begins with a question* runs a saying in the world of divination—those discoveries concern people's lives as well as spiritual and psychological ideas. This is the first thing I can promise you—that you will never say, "This is it. Now I have learned everything."

The second thing is that it will change you. If you truly give yourself to Tarot, throw yourself into it—the way Theresa Reed has done—it will teach you things: knowledge of psychology, magic, mystery, and Theresa's own favorite term, *intuition*. But it will also open up awareness you never knew you had, make you more attuned to the way people (yourself included) think and behave. And it will lead you into knowledge, from mysticism and ancient secrets to modern schools of psychology, from sacred doctrines to religious heresies, from magic to modern science, and back again (the back again is important). It does all this because Tarot is the world (there's a reason why the final card in the twenty-two Major Arcana cards is titled the World). To truly become a reader— maybe the only way to become a reader—is to embrace, well, everything.

There is a saying I've been following in my own teaching (it may be an old one, or I might have made it up—the great oracle, Google doesn't seem to know it). *What you love loves you.* Devote yourself to something and it will give you so much in return. Theresa Reed lives the Tarot. This is evident on every page. She *gives* herself to it. What is just as clear is how much the cards have given *her.*

Throughout the book, Theresa teaches by example. Her advice comes from many years of experience, with great stories to make it clear.

Consider one significant issue often discussed by Tarot readers—who says what in the course of a reading? Most of us have seen the extravagant claims of storefront psychics to "know all—tell all." One sign I remember seeing along the side of a main road in my area claimed "You say nothing! She says everything!" This, of course, is to reassure you the reader is a "genuine" psychic, not some charlatan. But the question remains— how *much* should the client say, and perhaps more, *when?*

As an aside—the person who gets the reading has had various titles over time. In earlier decades they were called *the sitter* because they usually sat down across from the reader (some modern readers have revived that term). A current expression is *seeker,* which might suggest the reader is a guru. And then there is the term often used in books, *querent.* Theresa prefers *client.* Her choice comes from the awareness that she is a dedicated professional, that this is not a hobby, or even a spiritual mission, but a business that she operates on the highest ethical level. This attitude, and life experience, comes through very strongly in the part of the book dedicated to developing your own practice as a Tarot reader.

So—what does the *client* say in a reading? Theresa begins by asking them what they want to know. She pays serious attention to what they say, sometimes suggesting a way to reframe the question. This is a common practice among readers, particularly when the issue concerns relationships, in particular the possibility of infidelity—in other words, cheating. If the client says, "I want to know if my boyfriend is cheating on me," the reader might suggest changing that to "What do you need to know about your relationship?" Or maybe, "How do honesty and fidelity figure in this relationship?"

But once the questions are set, and the cards laid out, Theresa prefers that the client not say anything until the end. This is because she reads *intuitively*—a very important word in this book—and intuition for Theresa depends on a kind of flow of information, insights, and impressions.

Does she suggest that we all do the same? I think she wants us to try out what she models for us, though not so precisely. She gives us ways to develop our own intuitive capabilities, and maybe she suspects many of us might end up following much of her approach. But she is modeling something for us, something really quite important that is worth considering, even if it goes against a reader's long-standing practice or a beginner's idea of what they think they want to learn. And yet, how we end up using what she gives us is up to us.

I'm sure that the last thing Theresa would want is to have legions of Reed-bots taking over the Tarot world. Instead, she shares her own experience, her skills and practical steps, but most of all her dedication, her love of Tarot and everything about it. She teaches us about service and, maybe especially, about joy.

Joy—and simply *fun*—is almost a guiding principle in this book. Even when Theresa is describing very "serious" matters, such as meditation or yoga as aids to releasing our intuitive abilities, she makes it clear we will have a great time doing these things. Many years ago, a spiritual teacher of mine named Ioanna Salajan told our class, "Nothing is learned except through joy," a statement and principle I have never forgotten. Theresa is a teacher, a businesswoman, and a community leader. But she is always first and foremost a reader, and the fact that she loves this life breathes on every page.

The book is roughly in two parts. The first concerns learning about the cards. Experienced readers may be tempted to skip this part, but I urge you to look carefully at Theresa's perspective and card meanings. They derive, after all, from dedication and years of practical experience. We can say something similar with her explanations of classic spreads (found at the end of the book), in particular the Celtic Cross. Many readers, maybe most, have used this spread, partly because it's so famous and partly because it really covers so many aspects of the client's/sitter's/querent's questions. But even if you have your own approach to the Celtic Cross, take a look at what Theresa says about it.

The second half of the book helps us develop that ability—skill—talent Theresa calls "intuition." There is endless debate in Tarot circles as to the difference between *psychic* and *intuitive* knowledge. Mary K. Greer says that intuition brings together available information at an unconscious level to come up with something surprising, while she reserves *psychic* for precise details that come to you from no clear source. Theresa tells the story of a reading where the name "Barry" suddenly came to her. Mary—and I—might label this psychic. (Or maybe we could call it telepathic, since the *client* obviously knew the name.)

For Theresa, the distinctions between all these things might be important to researchers or philosophers (or those of us who just love to ponder such things), but are ultimately not what really matters. At least not to a committed card reader. What matters for Theresa Reed is how much the reading helps the client. At the same time, she makes clear that not only can following her exercises and practices make you a better Tarot card reader, they're also exciting. Fun. Who wouldn't enjoy plucking the name "Barry" out of the air?

What this book teaches us is how to become a better Tarot reader. It does that through example as much as information. All the exercises, stories, card meanings, and techniques really serve one purpose. That is to follow Theresa's example and go beyond *learning* Tarot to *living* it.

—Rachel Pollack, author of *Seventy-Eight Degrees of Wisdom*

Introduction

The well-dressed man sat down at my tarot table and began shuffling cards. His face was a stone mask. He didn't want to give anything away. Not even a smile.

He studied my eyes for a moment and looked around my office, scrutinizing every detail intensely. I imagined that he was looking for some sort of trapdoor or magic trick—maybe a ghost. There was nothing of the sort. Just plain old me and my tarot cards.

After a long while, he put down the deck, cut the cards with his left hand per my instructions, and put them back together in a neat little pile. Once again, his face registered nothing. He sat back and crossed his arms, and I began to turn over the cards.

A story unfolded before me of lost love, challenges finding a new partner, and a job change that left him feeling displaced. Details began to emerge with each turn of a card, and I started looking at what might be ahead. A new position and better relationship were in the cards—once he made some changes. Those changes had to do with his anger problem, something he didn't like to acknowledge out loud but which seethed through his pores. (I think he was even mad that someone gifted him this tarot reading!)

I didn't ask him for confirmation, nor did I bother to look at him. I never look at the client when I read. I just kept turning over the cards and reading until I felt done. When that moment arrived, I looked up and asked, "Any questions?" The mask was gone, replaced by wide eyes and a trembling mouth.

"Uh . . . that was pretty amazing," he stammered, but then his eyes narrowed. "How do I know you didn't just Google me?"

"Since I didn't take your last name when I booked the appointment, that would be pretty impossible."

Mic drop.

His jaw was in his lap. He's been a client and a believer ever since.

My goal when I read tarot isn't to make anyone believe anything. My mission is always to help and guide. Tarot is my preferred tool for that. But those cards, much like any tool, need a power source to work well. My readings are powered by intuition.

I never had any formal training. For me, reading the cards came naturally because I'm a visual person, and I had the good fortune of growing up in a household that valued intuition. Omens and signs were something to be respected, not ignored. If Mom got one of her "visions," you'd better believe that something was up in the cosmos.

Everything was a sign.

I knew to pay close attention to those messages from the Universe before I even knew how to tie my shoes. So when I began my journey with tarot, it was easy for me to dive in, study the symbols, and intuit what they meant. Sometimes those meanings were not traditional interpretations.

One time, for example, I pulled the Five of Swords for a woman and warned her of a hostile takeover of her company, which she admitted was happening at the time of the reading. Another time I was doing a reading for a man about his father who had passed on, and the name I got as I turned over the Judgement card was "Barry." When I asked him who Barry was, his face blanched, and he said, "My uncle. He died a few months before my father."

How did I get that? Where does this information come from? How on earth can that be seen in a tarot deck?

In this book, we're going to explore the basics of intuitive tarot reading—how to read the cards in a perceptive, sensitive fashion. You'll learn about seeing patterns and clues in the images and what story they might be telling about the querent. Lots of little exercises and journaling prompts throughout the book will help you embody the energy of the cards, see the story they are telling, and learn to trust your gut (it's wiser than you think).

Plus, there's a chapter on going pro because, for some, this work may become a calling. If that's you, I want to show you the ropes so you can avoid the mistakes that I've made. I'm also a storyteller, so you'll find plenty of stories about my work that will help you get a glimpse into the real-life practice of someone who has read for the public for forty years (some of these are tales of horror!).

By the time you finish with this manual, you will be reading the tarot with full confidence in your instincts. No little white book necessary. Ready? Let's begin!

Blessings,

Theresa Reed

While all the stories in this book are true,
some names and identifying details have been changed
to protect the privacy of the people involved.

How to Use This Book

Tarot: No Questions Asked isn't just a book on tarot interpretations. While I do include a large chapter on card meanings, you will also find exercises called "Tarotcises" sprinkled throughout this book. These Tarotcises are lessons and experiments that I've used with students and in my own studies. You'll want to practice them because they will help you become proficient (plus, some of them will challenge you). Some of them might seem silly, but you should not underestimate their power. After all, learning through play is a way that many folks master a subject. The method doesn't always have to be "scholarly."

I've also loaded the book with journaling prompts because I have found that writing allows the information to seep into my subconscious and stay there. When I write things out, my brain is able to retain the info much better.

I encourage you to use this book up. Scribble in the margins, ponder the questions, test the Tarotcises on yourself and with others. Highlight what feels relevant and discard anything that doesn't. Find your own tarot voice (it doesn't need to sound just like mine).

We'll start out with the tarot basics first to form a foundation. The intuition part comes next, adding color and depth to your interpretations. Even if you think you don't have a psychic bone in your body, I've got methods to help you tap in. (Psst, tarot often helps people become more intuitive.) From there, we'll put this all together like a peanut butter and marshmallow fluff sandwich. The "Going Pro" chapter has insider tips that will help you set up shop with a minimum of fuss. This book is a full-on peek into how my tarot brain (and business) works and how I "live" tarot every day of my life.

A gentle reminder as you dive in: remain curious. Pay attention to your feelings. They will guide you brilliantly. That's the first step toward becoming a true intuitive tarot reader.

Gather Your Tools

As you begin your journey with me, you'll need a few proper tools. The first one: a tarot deck.

You can purchase yours at any online retailer that sells books or at your local metaphysical shop. Some stores have opened decks that you can peruse. This is nice because you can peek at the art and get an idea of how the cards feel in your hands. But if you don't have access to a shop, you can find lots of images online that may help you make your decision.

Frankly, I recommend that you start with the *Rider-Waite-Smith* tarot deck. It's a classic and the one you'll usually see featured in many tarot books, including this one. Plus, many modern decks are based on the same symbolism too.

Next, you'll want a journal. Journaling is an effective way to develop your intuitive and tarot skills. Keeping a record of your findings will help you grasp the information, but also you'll see patterns emerging and learn how your intuition is working and in what way. This will build confidence and greater awareness.

I have been keeping journals for intuition, tarot, and dreamwork for years. Writing down my insights not only allows the information to marinate in my bones but also gives me a record that I can reflect on later. Going back to my old notes can sometimes lead to aha moments, fresh insights, and validation. It can also help me see how I might have missed something . . . and that could lead to an entirely new interpretation.

Journaling helps connect the dots between tarot and intuition. In addition to consistent practice, journaling is the fastest way to gain confidence in your abilities.

Purchase a journal that makes your heart happy—one that you will love to fill with notes and sketches. For me, good paper and a solid cover are a must. I like to use pens, so I need paper that won't bleed. You might want to go digital, and while that option can work, I prefer the act of taking pen to paper. It seems to link the subconscious and conscious better than typing. Feel free to write in this book too.

Of course, some folks find that recording their voice works best. If you prefer that method, please follow your inclination. Only you know what is right for you. What's important isn't the way you journal but that you do.

You may want to have separate journals for tarot and intuition work. Or you can put your work all together in one. Again, what matters is that you find a system that allows you to be consistent.

Each day, take a few minutes to write in your tarot journal. Record dreams that you've had, signs from the Universe, or perhaps a tarot card for the day that you drew first thing in the morning as you sat down with your coffee. Jot down any impressions that come to mind. Work through the Tarotcises in this book. Don't stop and worry if you're right or wrong . . . or what things may mean. Just let your thoughts flow without stopping or censoring.

Once you've recorded your insights, put the journal away. Come back to it later in the day. Has anything unfolded that may correlate between your intuitive flashes or not? Did events manifest in a surprising way? What new insights have you gleaned? What, if any, patterns emerged?

Take time to add any notes or information that seems relevant.

Your tarot journal is a living, breathing record of your intuitive journey, one that you'll revisit again and again. Other than the tarot deck, it's also your best tool.

A Few Journaling Ideas

Card of the Day: I highly recommend pulling a card in the morning and journaling your thoughts. This is a practice I do every day. It's a way to deepen my connection to the cards and train my intuition to operate without a filter. I not only post a card of the day for myself but also put one online for my fans. This is also a good practice. There is something about putting a card out there for everyone to see that helps me grow more confident in my tarot skills. You might find that this routine does the same for you.

Date It: Always put dates on your journal entries. This way, you can look back and see how things unfolded . . . and how you grew as a tarot reader.

Draw: If you prefer, you might want to draw instead of write. You might draw an image from your dream or perhaps your own rendition of the card you pulled. This practice can also be a way to tap in. The reason is that our creativity comes from the same side of the brain as our intuition. If you feel called to draw, sketch, or paint, do it. Expressing yourself this way may be a better way for you to connect.

Scrapbook: You may also want to paste mini tarot cards, photos, or even small things you find throughout your day, such as feathers or clippings from magazines that capture your attention. Add ribbons, glitter, or whatever strikes your fancy; make your journal a creative, intuitive work of art!

Reflection: Every so often, go back to your old journals. Did your insights ring true? Or did you misinterpret something? Don't get bummed out if you think something didn't come true or make sense. Instead, write down what did transpire. Just the facts. Learn from that. Later on, you may discover that your original interpretations were valid but not the way you expected.

Remember: Intuition is not perfect. There is always room for misinterpretation. As you continue to practice, your instincts will get stronger. Like a muscle, instinct needs to be exercised regularly. The only way to become psychically fit is to work those intuitive muscles every day. Maintaining your journal is like doing bicep curls for your sixth sense!

PART ONE

Tarot Basics

Before You Toss that Little White Book . . .

"But Theresa, why do I need to know the meanings of the cards if I'm going to bypass that stuff and just trust my gut?" I know, it seems counterintuitive (pun intended). There is a reason why we are starting out with the bones.

Over the years, I've heard many well-meaning tarot teachers tell people to "throw away the little white book" and "read what you see!" To me, that's like throwing someone into the ocean before they can swim. Sure, some people quickly figure out how to float, but this approach isn't always wise. (True story: I fell through an inner tube in the middle of a lake and sank like a stone . . . and almost drowned. I never learned how to swim, and that incident guaranteed I would be too timid to try again.)

A better option is to begin with a solid foundation. For one, building the groundwork will give you confidence. But there's another reason: those traditional interpretations serve as a jumping-off point, a place to begin developing your own meanings. It's also mighty helpful to have those meanings memorized because you will have times when your intuition seems to be stuck on idle. When that happens, you can lean on those interpretations. Often, they will spur your instincts, and soon, your sixth sense will roar back to life.

Plus, you need to grasp what tarot is all about because reading without knowing the background and primary info is like driving a car without understanding what it runs on or where the steering wheel is located. Imagine someone asking you how many cards are in the deck, and you don't have an answer to that fundamental question. Nope! Not gonna happen on my watch!

A Wee Bit of History

You might want to know where tarot comes from. There are loads of myths around the origin of the cards! Some people believe they come from the Egyptians or the Romani. Other folks say that it's all some grand mystery. Nope to all of that.

In reality, the earliest tarot decks were discovered in Italy during the 1400s. They were hand-painted and depicted European nobility.

Playing cards predated tarot, and it's believed that tarot was initially created as a game too. (Fun fact: they are still played as a game in many parts of the world today.) Tarot was called *carte da trionfi* (cards of the triumphs), and then sometime about a hundred years later, they became known as *tarocchi*.

With the spread of mass printing presses in the 1500s, more people were able to get access. But it wasn't until the late 1700s that they became known for divination when a man named Jean Baptiste Alliete, also known as Eteilla (his last name spelled backward—it took me years to figure this out!), published one of the first books on tarot as a tool for divination. This put a whole new spin on the cards and increased their popularity. There is some scant evidence that tarot might have been used for divinatory purposes before then, but Eteilla's work put the esoteric and divination front and center.

Most of the earlier tarot decks were based on the Marseilles art. In the early 1900s, the mystic Arthur Edward Waite commissioned the artist Pamela Colman Smith to create the Rider-Waite-Smith deck, which is still the most popular deck to this day. The brilliance of this deck lies in the illustrated Minors, or pips, which made tarot as a divination tool way more accessible. Many modern tarot decks are based on the Rider-Waite-Smith's imagery. It's iconic. (This is also why I recommend it as the best starter deck for beginners. Once you can read with the RWS, you can read any deck!)

Here's another fun tarot history note: In *Tarot for Yourself*, Mary K. Greer writes: "The cards were used in a 16th-century poetry game called tarocchi appropriate that hints at character analysis. Someone dealt or assigned trump cards to each person (usually noble ladies), and then the poet improvised a sonnet matching the card and the characteristics of each person." Cool!

If you wish to learn more about Tarot's history, check out these books:

A Wicked Pack of Cards by Ronald Decker, Theirry DePaulis, and Michael Dummett

The Encyclopedia of Tarot, Vol. I & II by Stuart Kaplan

The Tarot: History, Symbolism, and Divination by Robert Place

Llewellyn's Complete Book of The Rider-Waite-Smith Tarot by Sasha Graham

Tarot Myths and Misconceptions

There are many myths and misconceptions about tarot. Let me bust a few of them right here, right now.

You must be gifted your first tarot deck. WRONG! If I had waited for that to happen, I might have never gotten my mitts on one! I grew up in a rural area, and it was only on one of those rare outings to the mall that I came face-to-face with a tarot deck! The other problem with this myth is that your taste may not be the same as someone else's. I've been gifted plenty of decks that I don't find attractive. Don't wait for someone else. Pick a pack you like; only you will know what that may be.

Tarot is evil. NOPE. Tarot is simply seventy-eight paper cards. Cards are not harmful. As with any tool, your intention is what dictates how they will be used. For example, a hammer can be used to hammer a nail and hang up a beautiful painting. But it can also be used to bludgeon someone.

The Death card means you're going to die. Unfortunately, this one seems to be perpetuated by popular culture. Often, you'll see a movie in which someone gets a tarot reading, and when that character pulls the Death card, the fortune-teller gasps and predicts doom and gloom. This is a stereotype, nothing more. The Death card indicates transformation. Predicting death is very complicated. The Death card on its own often has nothing to do with death.

You need to be psychic to read tarot. While you don't need to be psychic, a good connection with your intuition will strengthen your tarot reading skills. But get this: reading tarot will also power up your sixth sense. In short: they work together like peanut butter and jelly. Without calories.

You cannot read for yourself. SO wrong. This is the way most readers learn. Also: who knows you better than you?

Tarot can "see all." Tarot may be able to see a lot—and your intuition may too—but it's not infallible. Misinterpretation happens all the time. We're humans, after all. We don't always get it right, nor do we see every possible thing that might be creeping around the corner.

Keep in mind that you also have control over your future! Life doesn't just happen to you, and tarot isn't a passive act. Nothing is ever written in stone. If you don't like something that you see in the cards or the way something feels, you can change course at any time. As I always say: the cards tell a story, but you write the ending.

Can the cards predict the future? Yes, to an extent. They work sorta like this analogy: You're driving along at a good speed. Say you're going about fifteen miles over the speed limit. Suddenly, a car approaches you from the other direction. The driver blinks their lights. Most of us know what this means: either you forgot to turn on your headlights, or a police officer is ahead.

You check your headlights, and they are on. This means that the blinking lights must be a warning that a speed trap is waiting for you. You've been warned! Now you have a choice: You can continue zipping away like James Dean, and you can probably guess where this will end—getting pulled over and handed a ticket (or worse). You don't need to be psychic to see that outcome! But you also can choose to slow down. Take your foot off the gas. Maybe then, you might prevent that ticket from even happening in the first place.

Tarot for prediction works pretty much like that. It shows the possibilities as well as the problems. From there, it is up to you to use your common sense and free will to make smart choices.

Here's an example of the predictive process and how it can change depending on your decisions. I had a client named Leah who happened to be a drug dealer. She wasn't a dumb gal, but she just "fell into the life," as she would say, and didn't want to leave it because the money was too good. Leah would get a reading every so often to make sure she was in the clear and her "career" would continue to fund her lifestyle.

One day, she got a reading that didn't look favorable. The Justice card was in her environment, and the Five of Swords was in her future. "You're going to get caught. I think your neighbors are suspicious of you. Get a job—now—or you're going to be in deep trouble." She scoffed at the notion and left.

A few months later, the phone rang. I went to answer it and saw that the call was coming from the local jail. Usually, I would never pick up one of those calls, but for some reason, I felt compelled to do it this time. It was Leah. "Remember when you told me that my neighbor was suspicious? Well, it turns out my neighbor was a cop, and he busted me for dealing. Could you give me a quick reading?"

"When you get out and get your act together, I'll do it then," I said and hung up the phone. This whole situation could have been avoided if she had paid attention to the warnings and made better decisions. I'm happy to say that since that time, Leah has paid her dues and gotten her life on track. She's now a proud mama and holding down a great job. In a way, her jail time was the thing she needed to change course. So perhaps it was meant to be? I'd like to think so. But I'd also like to believe that this painful lesson could have been prevented too.

This story illustrates one of the beautiful things about tarot and intuition: Life is a series of choices. Our life doesn't just "happen to us." Our decisions dictate what sort of future unfolds. By paying attention to our choices, feelings, and the various signs around us, we can work with the Universe to create happy, healthy lives. Tarot and intuition are tools that anyone can use at any time for their benefit. Both help us to remain awake at the wheel, firmly in the driver's seat, moving toward a better destination.

Now that we've covered all that, let's look at the cards! The next section will give you interpretations for each card as well as exercises that I call "Tarotcises" and ways to embody the cards to find new, intuitive meanings.

Ready? Get your deck and let's go through it, card by card!

What's in the Deck?

A traditional tarot deck is composed of seventy-eight cards. You might encounter modern sets with extra cards. Frankly, I'm not a fan of those because I'm old skool. I take out the extras and stick with the seventy-eight. You might want to do that too . . . or not. Heck, if you feel those additional cards are going to add something to your readings, keep 'em. Otherwise, follow my cue and stick to the tried 'n true.

The tarot is divided into two sections:

Major Arcana

Minor Arcana

The Major Arcana cover the bigger picture, fated events, life's journey, and the significant lessons you may learn along the way. There are twenty-two cards in the Major Arcana, beginning with the Fool, which is numbered 0. Each image depicts an archetype that represents a step you might encounter on your spiritual path. Think of the Majors as the driving force to your evolution.

The Minor Arcana represent the day-to-day things that make up your life. Your job, relationships, finances, and struggles are depicted in the Minors. These are the things you can handle. There are fifty-six cards in the Minor Arcana.

In the Minor Arcana, there are four suits:

Wands

Cups

Swords

Pentacles

Each of these suits symbolizes a different facet of life:

Wands—Enterprise, creativity, work, passion

Cups—Emotions, relationships, love

Swords—Thoughts, conflicts, challenges

Pentacles—Finances, material goods, values

Each suit is also connected to an element:

Wands—Fire

Cups—Water

Swords—Air

Pentacles—Earth

You might want to consider the Major Arcana to be the element of spirit.

Let's explore the elements first.

Water—Cups

Water nourishes the soil and helps things grow. It pours, overflows, but can be stagnant too. Water can drown, but it can also dry up. Emotions can be like that too. Think about when your feelings are flowing beautifully. You forge deep connections, share your soul, fall in love, express your heart with vulnerability. But when your emotions get clogged, you can easily get hung up on the past. On the occasions when emotions overflow, they get the best of you and threaten to overwhelm. How do your feelings impact your life? In what way do you connect with others?

Play with the Water element and Cups: Lay out every card from the Cups suit in a row, from Ace to King. Examine how every figure interacts . . . or doesn't. Consider how the energy of a reading may feel if the majority were Cups. Would it tell a story of love . . . or emotions run amok?

Embody Water: Visit a lake, ocean, or other body of water. Sit at the edge and gaze out. Notice the ripples. Or, if it is still, peer in and look at your reflection. Take off your shoes and dip your toes into the water. Allow yourself to be quiet as you ponder how water feels. Then ask yourself: how deep can I go? Not into the water, but into the realm of emotions. Stand in a rain shower. Feel the droplets on your face. Allow yourself to get soaked to the bone. Inquire: How do my emotions impact my life? When have I totally immersed myself in my feelings?

Fire—Wands

Fire can heat up any situation. It warms your bones and helps you cook the food you eat. It can blaze trails and spark ideas or shed light. Fire creates movement and adventure. It's passion incarnate. Think about the flame that burns in your heart. What does it feel like when you're in love with a person or an idea? What can you build from that initial spark? Fire must always be handled with care. In the wrong hands, it can destroy what took a long time to create. It can extinguish an entire forest. Another side of this element is burnout—that feeling that happens when you give it your all and push beyond capacity. In this case, the flame dies because it cannot sustain that same level of heat. The Wands signify passion, the spark that creates movement, adventure, and work. How do intensity and devotion show up in your life? What are you building?

Play with the Fire element and Wands: Lay out all the cards from the Wands suit, from Ace to King. What passionate adventure can you see unfolding? If your reading was mostly Wands, would this indicate excitement or a situation that's ready to burn down?

Embody Fire: Light a candle. Soften your eyes and stare into the flame. Feel the warm glow as you bring the candle closer. Let your mind wander. Ask yourself: What lights me up? What brings intensity to my world? Then blow out the candle. Contemplate the times in your life when your dreams went up in smoke. What happens when you give up on your passions? What about when you go for them wholeheartedly?

Air—Swords

Air swirls around us. We are all breathing it in at the same time. It's continuously moving, even though we cannot see it. Air can be the force that moves a windmill. Swords are the realm of thoughts. Our thinking can be bold, exciting, or stifled. We can *fly*. Air can be thick and hard to breathe too. It can bring the storm that, in turn, clears the skies, but it can also whip things up and tear things down. Air needs grounding, or it can be unpredictable. The old saying "scattered to the four winds" means ideas that cannot be grounded. How do you channel your thoughts into action? In what way do you speak your truth?

Play with the Air element and Swords: Lay out every card from the Swords suit in order from Ace to King. What's the weather forecast? If you were a meteorologist and this was your fourteen-day forecast, what would you predict? If your reading was all Swords, would you see conflict or resolution?

Embody Air: Stand outside and feel the air on your face. Is it a cool breeze or a fierce wind? Allow the gusts to muss up your hair and spin you around. Breathe in deeply and exhale slowly. Think about how we're all breathing in the same air. Contemplate how that connects you to a family member or a stranger passing you on the street. Ask yourself these questions: How do my thoughts create connection . . . or conflict? When have my ideas inspired or created controversy?

Earth—Pentacles

Earth grounds us. It gives us something to stand on, and digging our toes deep into the dirt feels good. It's the soil upon which we plant our seeds, and we need it for growth. Think about how hard it is to cultivate anything in a desert. The lack of nutrient-rich dirt makes it impossible in some places. The earth regenerates itself and can heal. Pentacles is the material element of the tarot, the thing that makes life worth living and helps us create security. It's our roots. Those roots stabilize us. Earth shows us where we need to dig deep. But it can also be unyielding. In that case, nothing much happens. What do you value? Are you willing to get your hands dirty to make your dreams a reality?

Play with the Earth element and Pentacles: Once again, lay out all the cards from the Pentacles suit in a single line, from Ace to King. What's growing? What is the path to real security? If the reading was mostly Pentacles, would you see financial growth or something else?

Embody Earth: Take off your shoes and walk barefoot on the earth. Or dig your hands into the soil of a potted plant. Feel the terrain around you. Get sensuous with it. Smell that richness. Meditate on the wonder of the earth—how it sustains, heals, grows, replenishes. Ponder this question: What makes me feel secure? What can I create right now that might make a difference?

Elements Together

Think about how the elements might work together . . . or not. For example, Water and Earth show the potential for growth. After all, water replenishes the soil and creates the conditions for things to flourish.

On the other hand, Water and Fire create simmering energy that can make steam . . . or boil over. In some cases, water puts out the flame.

Air helps a fire to grow bigger. For example, when you're building a fire, blowing on the small flame creates a blaze. But wind can dry up earth, parching the surface and making the conditions unsuitable for farming.

Air and Water are neutral to each other. Same with Earth and Fire. That being said, anytime you see one element dominating, even in the case of compatibility, there is always the potential for things to become imbalanced. In a reading, look to see if the Minors are in harmony or if one is prominent.

This description provides a simplified version of elemental dignities, a tarot technique that derives interpretations based on how the elements of the cards go together . . . or not. If you want to learn more, you might want to check out *Tarot Decoded* by Elizabeth Hazel, which covers this technique in depth.

Order in the Court Cards

Within each suit of the Minor Arcana, there are four cards known as the Court cards. They can symbolize people in your life, opportunities you might be manifesting, as well as the energy you're transmitting or might need to bring to a situation.

Page—Young people, messages, seeds

Knights—Young people who identify as males, action, messengers

Queens—People who identify as females or feminine energy, mothering, nurturing

Kings—Mature people who identify as males or masculine energy, leadership, mastery

Do not get overly concerned with gender. Anyone at any time can operate with male/female energy. The King of Pentacles doesn't automatically guarantee some tall, dark stranger is about to waltz into your life. This card could indicate that you need to take responsibility for your finances instead!

How do you know which meaning is which? The interpretation all comes down to the context of the question and the position of the card. For example, if someone is asking about their business and the Queen of Pentacles shows up, this card might be a sign that the querent needs to focus on the financial aspect of the company. The Knight of Cups in the near future position might indicate a romantic partner on the horizon for someone who is wondering about meeting someone new. Two Pages in a general outlook could signal a time when the querent is developing new projects . . . or is pregnant with twins.

Getting the hang of the Court cards takes time, but with enough practice, you'll start to see when it's a person, message, or advice for the querent. If you want to learn more, I recommend that you check out *Understanding the Tarot Court* by Mary K. Greer and Thomas Little.

Tarotcise

I always recommend that beginners create avatars for each Court card based on a celebrity or someone they know. This is a mnemonic device, a memory aid that will help your brain remember the energy of each figure.

Now that you understand the basic structure of the deck, let's gather some possible interpretations. The tarot card meanings in this manual are meant to be general guidelines. The longer you read, the less you need to rely on these interpretations. For now, though, lean on them. Refer back to the book as much as you need.

When you're starting out, you might need to refer to the book all the time. That's fine. Keep going. Soon, you'll be able to read the cards without glancing at the book. But until then, these interpretations will help you navigate tarot with a bit more confidence . . . like a set of tarot training wheels! No shame in that! (Psst, we all started out this way!)

In addition to interpretations for each card, you'll notice journaling prompts, Tarotcises, and a section called "How to embody the energy of this card." Each of these elements will help you connect with the tarot in different ways.

The journaling prompts are designed to get you thinking about what the cards might mean to you. The Tarotcises challenge you to explore different ways of looking at the cards. The "embody" parts allow you to bring tarot into your everyday experiences and feel the energy of the cards, essential for understanding the meaning. I recommend doing all three for each card for a full, rich experience.

A Word about Reversals

If you want to see tarot people argue, ask their opinion about reversals. Some readers hate them. Others think they are essential (and that people who don't use them are lazy). For myself, I didn't realize that some people didn't use them until much later in my career.

I have always worked with reversals. In my opinion, they can add subtle nuances to a reading. *But* I've had plenty of great readings from folks who didn't bother with them. Really, it's up to you.

When you're first starting out, you might want to leave them alone. That's fine. But once you get going and feel confident with uprights, give them a try. You might find that they take your readings in exciting new directions.

Reversals can signal blocked energy or something stalled. You can also look at them as the opposite meaning of the card. For example, the Devil reversed may imply a release from something that is binding you. Liberation time, baby!

Keep in mind that whatever card you're looking at, when upside down, it's not in its element. The vibe is unsteady, blocked, or the opposite. One technique that I like is to look at the upright version of the card as advice. For example, if you pull the Hermit reversed, it might be a sign that you need to take time out to contemplate your situation. The Three of Cups reversed might say you need to blow off some steam and hang with your friends . . . or to seek support from your buddies. The solution is in the upright version! Shazam!

My friend Shaheen Miro likes to turn the reversed card upright as a way to "move the energy." I love this idea. If you pull a reversal for yourself or another person, turn it upright. How does that feel? Be curious. Turn it back upside down. What do you see now? Does it feel different? Once again, turn it around. Think about how that energy might be moving forward if you make a change. Tarot is so magical!

The Major Arcana

To recap: The Major Arcana are the bigger picture, fate, and the important lessons that help you grow. There are twenty-two cards in the Major Arcana, beginning with the Fool, which is numbered 0. You can easily figure out which cards are Majors as you peruse the deck: they have a Roman numeral at the top and a title such as "The Magician" on the bottom.

Got that? Awesome. Let's dig in!

THE FOOL.

The Fool

Card Number 0

URANUS

The Fool steps forward, face tilted to the sky, oblivious to the fact that he might be stepping over a cliff. He carries a bag attached to a wand, which symbolizes his past experiences and potential. He's moving forward, without a care in the world, open to any and all adventures that might be coming his way. His faithful companion, a little white dog, nips at his heels. Is the dog warning him that he's about to go over the edge? Or is the dog happy to join him for this wild ride?

This card symbolizes a new phase in life, a journey, risk, and innocence. It's a sign that now you must take a brave leap of faith, even if you're not sure where you will land. Instead, remain open to what's ahead and trust that this path may lead you in an exciting new direction. The Fool always walks where angels fear to tread.

Other ways of looking at this card: living in the moment, taking a new route, a spiritual journey, innocence, lack of worldly experience, trusting in the goodness of the Universe, a minimalist lifestyle, doing what's totally unfamiliar, the "beginner's mind."

The reversed Fool pulls back from the ledge. Instead of leaping forth with total trust and love, he's hesitant. Fearful. Not ready to take the plunge. In a divinatory reading, this reversal says: You must look before you leap. Or maybe not take that chance at all. This can also symbolize your abandoning a situation . . . or your inability to trust your instincts.

While caution and fear are typical interpretations, the other side of this card is reckless behavior. That person who drinks too much and insists on driving home only to get pulled over and thrown in jail? That is the Fool reversed in action.

How to embody the energy of this card: Take a deep breath and do something entirely out of your comfort zone. Karaoke is perfect! Stepping onto a stage with the risk of feeling foolish—that's the Fool in a nutshell. Grab a sensible pal (your own version of the little white dog), hit the local karaoke spot, and sing your hearts out!

A question to ponder: *What is the biggest risk you've ever taken?*

Tarotcise

 Sit with the Fool card for a few minutes. Which symbol stands out? Take out your journal and begin to riff on that symbol. Make a note of anything that comes to mind. Let your words flow without stopping to edit. Just write what you feel. Put this away and then reflect on your words at a later date. What did you uncover? What kind of connection did you make to this card?

THE MAGICIAN.

The Magician

Card Number 1

MERCURY

Unlike the Fool, the Magician knows what he's doing. He's standing fully in his power, tools laid out in front of him, ready to manifest something big. With one hand raised to the sky and the other pointed to the earth, he embodies "As above, so below." The Magician is focused willpower, the kind you need when you're upping your game . . . or pulling a rabbit out of your hat. (Tricks aren't only for kids.)

The Magician indicates committing to a goal and using all of your resources to make magic happen. Everything you need is present. Focus on what you want to create, have, or be, and know that nothing can stop you. When this card comes up in a tarot reading, it says: You've got this. Go ahead now and make epic stuff happen. It's up to you.

Keep in mind, the Magician can indicate trickery or sleight of hand. Is there mischief afoot? Are you operating fair and square? Or looking for a shortcut?

In some readings, this card can advise keeping your eyes on the prize and your integrity in check. Pay attention to which other cards surround this one, and you'll be able to see if the Magician is on the up and up . . . or up to no good.

Other ways of looking at this card: potential, taking action, strength, creativity, a masculine approach to matters, a miracle.

The reversed interpretation of this card symbolizes a lack of talent and/or resources. It's also a sign that the focus isn't here. Instead of being able to manifest your goal, things fall flat. Incompetence leads to failure. Willpower becomes weak, or in some cases, it turns into an abuse of power. You may resort to bullying or other aggressive methods to attain your end. Instead of taking responsibility, you pass the buck on to someone else. The other way to look at this reversal is overconfidence. That person who thinks he can pass the test without bothering to study? No one is surprised when that guy gets an F.

How to embody the energy of this card: Set a goal for yourself and then stay on it until the deed is done. You can pick something simple such as cleaning out your closet or something else you're good at. Once you've decided what your goal will be, set a timer and then go for it! Enjoy that feeling of directing your will and making something magical happen, even if that wizardry is simply a decluttered closet.

A question to ponder: *What is your superpower?*

Tarotcise

Take the Magician card out of the deck and ask yourself this: what is trying to manifest in my life today? Sit quietly with your eyes closed and notice any symbols or words that come into your mind. How do they make you feel? Does one seem to stand out? Open your eyes and write down anything that seems relevant. Over the next few days, notice if something shows up in your life that appears to be connected to this exercise. For example, you may get an image of a fountain pen in your mind. Later in the week, a handwritten note from your best friend arrives in the mail.

The High Priestess

Card Number 2

MOON

An aura of mystery surrounds the High Priestess. This lovely lady is decked in blue and holding a secret scroll. What might that scroll contain? Only a hint is revealed: TORA. Some say that this might be the Torah. Others say it's a symbol of hidden knowledge, secrets that only she holds. She has a moon under her feet and sits in front of a curtain, which shows a hint of a river flowing in the background. Both are symbols of the subconscious. Right away, you know one thing: she's deep.

The High Priestess represents feminine wisdom and intuition. When this card arrives in a tarot reading, the message is simple: Follow your gut. Listen to that small, still voice within. Your own inner guidance is all that you need. Do not seek answers from others; instead, look to your own wisdom.

This card can also symbolize Yin or the passive qualities of power. There is no need to take action. This time may require you to kick back and allow. See what unfolds. Trust that everything is moving in divine order.

The High Priestess also references secrets. Some things are not meant to be revealed at this time. That will come later when the time is right.

Other ways of looking at this card: shape-shifter, mystery, initiation, a feminine approach to a situation, the unknown, female concerns, look beneath the surface, fertility.

When the High Priestess is reversed, she's no longer looking within; she's concerned with the outer world. Instead of passivity, the energy is active. Involved. Downright passionate. But do know that this reversal can also symbolize the failure to listen to your better instincts. Remember that time when you knew you shouldn't take that route, but you did, only to end up in the middle of nowhere? That's High Priestess reversed.

How to embody the energy of this card: Pay close attention to how you feel every time you make a decision. Do you go with your logic? Or your gut? Try experimenting with both. See how often your instincts steer you in the right direction, even when common sense might suggest otherwise. Another great way to take on the energy of the High Priestess is to practice stillness. Withdrawal from the hubbub of daily life is a fantastic way to get your balance back . . . and to hear your inner wisdom. Shhhh. . .

A question to ponder: *When has your intuition proven to be amazingly accurate?*

Tarotcise

 Hold the High Priestess in your hands and soften your gaze. As you focus on the card, begin to visualize what's behind the curtain. What is happening behind the scenes? What do you feel? If you can't see through the curtain, what might your intuition tell you about what's in the background? Let your imagination and intuition run wild!

THE EMPRESS.

The Empress

Card Number 3

VENUS

Let's now move on to the next female in the Major Arcana: the Empress. One look at her sitting back comfortably on her throne and you can see that she's large and in charge! She is female power in all its lush glory. The lavish gown, crown of stars, fluffy pillows, flowing river, and golden wheat field say prosperity, pleasure, all the good things.

When you're interpreting this card, abundance is the key. This is the card of plenty—a sign that everything you're working on is bearing sweet fruit. The rewards are coming in at last. What you touch can turn to gold. Like the figure in this card, you can create whatever you want. All the powers of the Universe are with you.

Because this card is connected to fertility, it can indicate motherhood, pregnancy, or birth. Marriage and commitment also fall under this card's realm.

The Empress is focused on nurturing. Whether she's taking care of her family or nurturing a goal, you can be sure she's putting all of her attention into the task. Therefore, this card can advise you to take good care of those who are under your wing or to whatever you are looking to create.

One more thing! This card can also represent sensuality. Time to indulge in some pleasurable activities? Uh-huh. Boom chicka wow wow!

Other ways of looking at this card: tenderness, wealth, a big harvest, Mother Earth, connecting with nature, beauty.

So when you reverse the Empress, what might you learn about her? For one, the pleasure principle comes to a grinding halt. That lusty passion becomes subdued or is gone altogether. The fertility dries up, and now you're looking at a barren field where nothing much can grow. The need to nurture is replaced with indifference or cruelty. The overprotective mother who doesn't allow her child to fly the nest can be the negative expression of this card.

However, this is not all bad; sometimes the Empress reversed indicates a time when you need to pull back from your emotions and all that pleasure. Instead of being all about feelings, it's time to get into your head. The sensual gets replaced with the logical.

In some cases, this reversal can also indicate overindulgence. If you're overdoing the good life, don't be surprised if it bites back in the future.

How to embody the energy of this card: The Empress favors a sensual approach to life. One way to get that is by doing something pleasurable—a feast for the senses. That could be a self-care activity such as getting a massage or indulging in a decadent meal with your partner à la *9½ Weeks*. Whatever you do, make it passionate and sumptuous.

A question to ponder: *What do you need to nurture right now?*

Tarotcise

 Compare the High Priestess to the Empress. When you put these two tarot ladies side by side, what differences can you see? What similarities? Now, take a moment to ponder the reversed meanings. Notice anything? When you turn these two around, you'll see that they both hold the mirror image of the other. The High Priestess reversed moves out of passivity and becomes passionate while the Empress reversed steps inward and pulls back.

The Emperor

Card Number 4

ARIES

The mighty Emperor sits on his stone throne, eyes darting from side to side, alert for signs of trouble. He holds a scepter in his one hand and an orb in the other. As you peek beneath his robe, you may notice he's wearing armor. He's ready to lead, invade, or protect his kingdom. Unlike the Empress, the Emperor has nothing soft about him.

The Emperor is the patriarch of the tarot world, the father figure who heads the household or the kingdom. He's power personified and all about authority. When he shows up in a tarot reading, you know that things are about to get real serious, real quick. This card demands a disciplined approach. Silliness won't cut it.

Therefore, a possible interpretation is hard work and discipline. This reading could signal a time when you need to take a somber approach to a situation. If you're willing to do the work now, you'll be laying a secure foundation for the future.

The Emperor can also indicate authority, as in dealing with authority figures. That could be the boss, Dad, or the law. Whether you're playing the role of the ruler or you are under someone else's rulership, respect is needed.

In some readings, this card could indicate a period of security ahead. Things are where they need to be, and you can rest easy. The foundation is as solid as a rock. You can depend on current circumstances to be stable.

Other ways of looking at this card: regulation, routines, support, order, organization, control, leadership, strength, law, making rules, boundaries, government, sternness, protector.

When the Emperor is reversed, it can bring out a softer side to this card. Instead of being Mr. Stern, he's a bit more chill. Less concerned with ruling things, he's more apt to allow everyone to do their thing.

The card can also indicate someone who is losing their grip or power. Instead of everything being under control, everything is falling apart. This is the crumbling empire, the politician who gets overthrown by angry subjects, or the CEO who gets ousted in a hostile takeover.

The Emperor reversed can also symbolize trouble with authority figures. Think James Dean lipping off to his dad in *Rebel Without A Cause*. That.

This card reversal can also suggest immaturity. Instead of finding the courage to do the right thing, the person runs from responsibilities. The deadbeat dad is the perfect example of the Emperor reversed.

How to embody the energy of this card: Set a goal for thirty days. Thirty days is often the right time to make a habit stick. Let's say your goal is to give up your daily coffee habit. I know, I know—that's not an easy one! Now stick with it for the next thirty days. Channel the disciplined energy of the Emperor. At the end of the thirty days, give yourself a pat on the back for a job well done.

A question to ponder: *Where do you need more order?*

Tarotcise

 The Emperor is such a severe dude. For this Tarotcise, try to find something soft about him. Study the card carefully. Where might you find tenderness in the Emperor?

THE HIEROPHANT

The Hierophant

Card Number 5

TAURUS

Of all the cards in the Major Arcana, the Hierophant was the hardest one for me to grasp. From the funky name that took me forever to learn how to pronounce to the religious garb, call me confused. Only after spending a lot of time with this card was I able to come to terms with it. Interestingly, I have come across a lot of other tarot readers who tell me the same thing; they just didn't jive with this guy. But he's really not so bad once you get used to him!

For one, the Hierophant isn't about religion per se, although in some interpretations this card can indicate religion, rites, dogma, or doctrines. I remember reading for a young woman years ago, and this card landed in the position marked "environment." I asked her if there was a religious person in her household. She said her father was a preacher. So yes, the card can indeed have something to do with religion.

It's also a card that favors rules and order. When this card turns up in a tarot reading, it says: Obey the rules. Don't buck the system. The status quo must be upheld. While the Emperor makes the laws of man, the Hierophant creates the laws of the spiritual realm.

The Hierophant can also indicate a time when an orthodox approach might be the best solution. Conforming to society's rules may be needed. For example, visiting an attorney for a divorce might be a better plan than "conscious uncoupling" for some couples.

This card can also represent a teacher, mentor, counselor, or wise elder who plays an essential role in your life. This person may be presenting you with critical teaching. Pay attention and pay your respects too. Often, I interpret this card as the "therapy" card because sometimes people need guidance from a sage therapist that they can trust.

Other ways of looking at this card: conformity, groupthink, studies, rituals, ceremonies, benediction, the Establishment, joining an organization or movement, secret knowledge, tradition, blind obedience.

When the Hierophant is reversed, it favors bucking the trends. Instead of following the rules, now it's time to do your own thing. Follow your own drumbeat and feel free to chuck the standard way of doing things. An unorthodox approach is the best way forward.

Reject traditions and find new ideas, structures, and ways of thinking. Nonconformity all the way! What's important here is that you examine and create your own belief system rather than blindly go along with someone else's. Obedience is not necessary.

The other thing to keep in mind is that this card can symbolize abuse of power, such as a cult leader—someone who preys on people's spiritual beliefs for their own gain.

In some cases, the Hierophant reversed could signal rebellion or anarchy. Put this with the Tower, and a full-scale revolution is underway!

How to embody the energy of this card: Because this card can be connected to religion, a great way to integrate this card might be to attend a spiritual service. Visit a church or temple, join a meditation group, chant in an ashram, light a candle in a rectory, or hang with your local Pagans. See how it feels to be part of a religious ceremony.

A question to ponder: *What role has religion played in your life?*

Tarotcise

 Both the Emperor and the Hierophant are concerned with obeying the rules. What rules might these two share? How might they view rules differently? If they could talk, what rules would they be stating? Take a few minutes to consider these questions and then journal your thoughts. Lastly, focus on this: if you were an Emperor or leader of a religious group, what rules would you create, and how might you enforce them?

THE LOVERS.

The Lovers

Card Number 6

GEMINI

I swear that the Lovers card is the one that everyone *wants* to see in a tarot reading. After all, romance is one of the most common topics in tarot! Not many people ask about love and hope for a "bad" card; they want the Lovers, front and center.

And why wouldn't they? The image is straight out of the Garden of Eden with the naked couple and the flaming angel floating above them. It's paradise in a tarot card!

The Lovers card symbolizes relationships—not just romantic ones, mind you. This card can indicate any important partnership, including a joint business venture. In questions about amour, it's a sign that love is on the way and a commitment is possible. For biz or other types of relationships, the Lovers card alludes to people uniting in a spirit of harmony. The energy here is one of mutual attraction, with the ability to forge a deep connection. Whether you're coming together for romance or to seal a deal, you can be sure that things will be moving in the right direction when this card turns up. Help is available, and the support you need is right there, under your nose.

This card can also indicate choices, as in a major decision. If you are contemplating making a big move, this card says: consider the consequences carefully and let your higher guidance dictate the way.

Other ways of looking at this card: union, balance, shared values, intimacy, attraction, sex, vulnerability, temptation, an ethical crossroads, torn between right and wrong.

When you turn the Lovers upside down, it's a sign of a relationship gone awry. Instead of that healthy balance, the energy here is destructive. This is the card of bad romance, a doomed marriage, or a relationship that goes off the rails due to a breach of trust. It can also symbolize a partnership where one person puts more into it than the other. That classic commitment-phobe who strings you along? Yup: Lovers reversed. This reversal can also indicate an addictive relationship, especially when paired with the Devil. That toxic couple who are on-again off-again and fueled by sex and violence—Lovers reversed again.

Lovers reversed can also symbolize making poor choices. Instead of letting your higher self lead the way, you're tempted by all the wrong things. The angel and devil are fighting on your shoulders . . . and the devil is winning.

How to embody the energy of this card: Artist Marina Abramović did a live performance piece in which she sat in total silence with strangers for one full minute. It was raw, intense, and vulnerable. Total Lovers energy. Find someone you can practice this with. Sit with them face-to-face. Be totally present with them as they are. You may feel a bit silly at first, but stay with it. Be open, vulnerable, and in the moment.

A question to ponder: *How do you show up in your relationships?*

Tarotcise

 Pull out the Hierophant and the Lovers. You'll notice that they have a similar structure—a spiritual figure with two people below them. How might these two cards be the same? How might they be different? If you could imagine the advice the spiritual figures might give, what would the angel say, and how might that be different or the same from the pope's counsel? Journal your answers.

THE CHARIOT.

The Chariot

Card Number 7

CANCER

The Chariot always conjures up images of Spartacus, the Thracian gladiator who escaped during a major slave revolt. In a famous scene from the film starring Kirk Douglas, the Romans are trying to locate him by offering up a pardon for anyone who might identify Spartacus. All of the men respond with "I am Spartacus," which pretty much helps the real dude hide. It's an epic movie, and this is an epic card.

The Chariot implies that a victory is at hand. Through sheer drive and willpower, you're able to direct your fate toward the finish line. The reins are in your hands, and you've found the perfect vehicle to reach your goal. You're in control, baby. Not much will get in the way. Even if there are some potholes or contradictions, you've discovered the secret detour and progress is assured. Success is yours for the taking. Giddyup!

Other ways of looking at this card: intention, sustained effort, fixating on a goal, determination, military, combat, strength, ego, taking control, confidence, travel. On a mundane level, this card can indicate your vehicle.

But what happens when the Chariot is overturned? For one, obstacles are in the way. Suddenly, the path is no longer clear. The goal becomes unattainable, and you're stuck with your wheels spinning, going nowhere fast. Or it's possible that you've lost sight of your goals or are giving up. The willpower needed to reach your destination has been lost. Instead of sitting in the driver's seat and cruising toward a sweet finish, you're lost or heading for a crash. In some cases, the reversed Chariot can indicate misplaced willpower or an abuse of power. Road rage is a perfect example of this card gone amok.

How to embody the energy of this card: Because the Chariot is all about willpower, you'll want to focus on that aspect of this card. An excellent way to do that is through *trataka*, or concentrated gazing with a candle. Find a quiet place where you will not be disturbed. Light the candle. Gently gaze at the flickering flame. Keep your focus there for a few minutes. Watch the interplay of light and shadow. See the image of the fire soften and dissolve. Try to keep your attention entirely on the candle, even if there are distractions around you. Stay at this effort for about five minutes or more. Notice how this practice calms the mind and brings you right into the present moment. The present moment is where willpower flourishes.

A question to ponder: *If you could go anywhere in the world, where would you go and how might you arrive at your destination?*

Tarotcise

 Pick a movie that is all about ambition and triumph. Of course, I recommend *Spartacus*. As you watch the drama unfold, think about the Chariot. When did the main character find the perfect vehicle? What were the different moving parts they needed to control? Or what aspects of their own personality did they need to manage? What obstacles did they overcome? See the movie though the eyes of the Chariot.

Strength

Card Number 8 (in some decks 11)

LEO

On the Strength card, a woman is closing the jaws of a mighty lion. She has a look of total calm on her face. The lion looks up at her with trust. There is no struggle present, although you would think that taming a lion would require some sort of tussle. Instead, you can see grace under pressure—the perfect interpretation for this card.

The Strength card isn't necessarily about physical strength, although in some cases, it can be. Instead, this is the inner strength that is needed to overcome great obstacles. Some of those obstacles can be internal, such as taming the inner demon or the ego. (Remember, the Lion is connected to the Sun sign Leo, which rules the ego.) When you're dealing with any issue, the Strength card is a reminder that these things can be handled with a firm but gentle touch. Face your problems head-on, trusting that you have what it takes to come out on the other side, stronger and wiser. No matter what is in front of you, what's inside of you will pull you through.

Other ways of looking at this card: calmness, survival skills, boundaries, guardian angel, persuasion, courage, patience, mastery of a situation.

The reversed Strength card implies weakness—both physical and emotional. In the physical realm, the divinatory meaning is feeling weak and having low energy reserves. This would say it is time to pull back and take a breather. Recoup so that you can gather more strength. If you are looking at a situation that is not health-related, this would indicate cowardice or not having the wherewithal or optimism to see things through. Instead of taking control, the figure gives up. The Strength reversed could also symbolize being overcome by inner demons. Pair this with the Devil card, and you see the full-fledged addict, tormented by addictions but unable or unwilling to give them up.

How to embody the energy of this card: The next time you find yourself facing a significant issue, take a moment to tap into your own inner strength. Find those reserves of power within yourself (yes, they are there). Tell yourself, "I've got this." Because you do.

A question to ponder: *When have you felt stronger than your challenges?*

Tarotcise

Both the Strength card and the Magician have the infinity symbol, or lemniscate, above their heads. This is a symbol of endless energy. How is the power of the Strength card different from the Magician's? How is it the same?

THE HERMIT.

The Hermit

Card Number 9

VIRGO

Sometimes you need to be alone. It's the only way you can find the answers. That's the energy of the Hermit. On this card, the figure stands high on a mountaintop, far away from the noise of the world, with only a lantern to light his way and a staff to lean on. Does he feel alone? We'll never know. But one thing's for sure: he's taking a break so that he can figure things out.

When the Hermit shows up in a tarot reading, this card symbolizes the withdrawal from the outer world. Instead of being part of everything, he is stepping away so that a better, clearer perspective can be discovered. This is the internal journey, with little connection to the externals. The externals only serve as a distraction from the truth. That truth can be accessed only by shutting out all the noise.

Sometimes this card can represent a teacher or guide of sorts, someone who can help you access those hidden answers that are locked inside. Think of a wise guru or spiritual leader who might impart necessary wisdom during a dark time. They illuminate the path ahead. This can be someone you work with, or you may be the one playing that role for someone else. Sometimes you need to be your own wise teacher too. After all, if you spell out *guru*, you get *G-U-R-U*: gee, you are you.

Other ways of looking at this card: introspection, recluse, introvert, retreat, seeking wise counsel, seclusion, the seeker.

Now when this card is reversed, the energy becomes wholly externalized. The outside world leads the way, and this reversal says: be part of that. No more hiding away! It's a time to return to the outer life—or to a situation that needs your presence. Sometimes the only way to gain wisdom is by repeating a mistake or dealing directly with a mess you don't like. The Hermit reversed warns of learning the same lesson all over again, but as the saying goes, sometimes the only way to learn is the hard way.

Another interpretation of this reversal is the fear of other people. The agoraphobic or person who wants to hide from the world? That's the Hermit reversed. It can also symbolize escapism. A refusal to deal with problems. Instead of handling the issues, the person runs from these problems or refuses to take responsibility. Immaturity and a refusal to grow up are both energies consistent with this reversal. I like to think of this card as another "deadbeat dad" of the tarot world—not willing to pony up. Rather than pay his dues, he takes off. He's probably hitting the road with the reversed Emperor!

How to embody the energy of this card: Go on a mini-sabbatical. Take a day off from the world. No internet, television, or contact with anyone. Unplug from it all. Spend the whole day in silence. Rest, read, meditate, ponder. Notice how much clearer and calmer you feel after a day at the hermitage.

A question to ponder: *What role does stillness play in your life?*

Tarotcise

The lantern symbolizes a guide that helps find the way in the dark. Go through the tarot deck and look for the cards with "dark" backgrounds. What light might the Hermit's lamp shed on these cards? What wisdom might he glean from going into the scenes that are playing out? For example, the Ten of Swords is a rather glum card with a jet-black background. When the Hermit brings his lamp to the situation, he might draw attention to the lack of bloodshed. He might point out the sunrise in the background and the hand held in the jnana mudra, a yogic hand position that symbolizes wisdom. Instead of loss and betrayal, that lamp shows a blessed ending that is less painful than imagined and the light at the end of this tunnel just on the horizon. Try that with other "dark" cards and see what you might discover.

WHEEL of FORTUNE.

The Wheel of Fortune

Card Number 10

JUPITER

The Wheel of Fortune, a symbol-rich card, is often a happy one to see in a tarot reading, for it indicates a change is on the way . . . and usually a good one at that. This is the card of fate, a sign that nothing is going to remain the same.

As you begin to study the card, you can easily get taken in by all those moving parts: the sphinx, angel, phoenix, bull, lion, snake, and jackal-headed creature seem to guard the wheel in some fashion or another. What role do they play? How might they be turning the wheel or going along for the ride?

Let's take a peek at some of these guys before moving on to interpretations. The Sphinx sits atop the wheel and holds a sword in his hand. This is the guardian of all the secrets—fate itself. The four creatures on the outside of the wheel also show up in card number 21, the World. They represent the four elements or fixed signs of the zodiac. Attached to the wheel is a snake, a symbol of transformation, and that jackal-headed creature, Anubis, is the leader of dead souls. As you can see, the theme here is of fate, change, death, and rebirth.

Right away, the theme alerts you that this card indicates a pivotal shift, a significant change ahead, and the end of a cycle. What prompted the change or what it's about may not be clear, but one thing is for sure: this change is necessary and for the better. That old saying "everything happens for a reason" might be a perfect analogy for the Wheel of Fortune. Sometimes things just happen, and you don't know why, but upon later reflection, you can see how important those changes were. So when this card arrives, roll with it. Put yourself in fate's hands and trust that things are moving along as they should. Do not fear change; initiate it if possible. Karma is doing its thang. Don't like how it's working out? Remember that your past deeds have set the wheel in motion. The changes happening are part of a karmic cycle, and you gotta move with it as best as you can.

Other ways of looking at this card: destiny, consequences of past actions, movement, new directions, turning things around, luck, breakthrough, taking a chance.

The reversed Wheel of Fortune can represent limbo or a time when things seem to be up in the air. The forward motion is now stuck on auto-pilot, and all you can do is wait things out. This can also symbolize a refusal to accept the changes. Instead of going with the flow, a struggle ensues. At times, this card can also indicate a reversal of fortune; suddenly everything falls apart, and the wheel comes to a grinding halt. Past actions have created the conditions for failure. Time to start over from scratch. Bad luck or bad decisions? Only time will tell.

How to embody the energy of this card: Because the Wheel of Fortune signifies change, one of the best ways to feel this card is by setting your own wheel in motion. You can do that by setting an intention. Take out your journal and think about a change you'd like to see in your life. Visualize what that might look like or how you might feel if that change happened. Take a minute to jot down an affirmation that best represents you once your goal has been reached. For example, if you want a new job, your declaration may be: "I have the perfect job." Once you've decided on your affirmation, write down a few things you're willing to do to make that happen. Using our example, that might be: "Polish off my resume. Search online. Make phone calls to prospective employers."

Next step: put your journal away and start taking at least one of those actions. A few months later, revisit your notes and see what changes have occurred. Did you reach your goal? If not, what new wheel must you set in motion?

A question to ponder: *When has fate intervened on your behalf?*

Tarotcise

If you look around the wheel, you'll notice the letters T-O-R-A—the same letters on the scroll the High Priestess holds. What might this tell you about that scroll? Bonus: compare the four figures on this card with the ones on the World card. What clues do these characters hold for each card?

Justice

Card Number 11 (in some decks 8)

LIBRA

Like the Wheel of Fortune, Justice deals with karma. Both cards indicate that what you're experiencing at this time is mostly due to past actions. The consequences have now come fully due. The key to this card is to understand the truth of the past. When you can fully comprehend and take personal responsibility for your role in past events, you will see the positive manifestation of this card. Unwilling to do that? Well, Justice will be present, but you may not like it.

I'll never forget the time long ago when I was a bartender slinging drinks and tarot. I read for a skeptical patron who thought it was all malarkey. As he sipped his beer, I laid out the cards, and Justice came up along with a few not-so-pleasant-looking cards. I looked at him and said, "Whatever you're doing, change course. If you don't, you're going to get into trouble with the law." He scoffed at me, finished his drink, tossed a tip on the bar, and told me that I was dead wrong.

A few weeks later, he was arrested for stealing cartons of cigarettes off trucks. He had been running a game where he lifted them and then sold them to people for a cheap rate for years. The jig was up, and he ended up serving time. One of his friends came to the bar a few days after this happened and told me that the tarot reading had haunted the man. Although the guy I read for had put on a brave, cocky face in front of the other bar patrons and me, behind the scenes, he kept asking his friend, "You don't think that tarot reader is right, do you?" It wasn't long before he got his answer.

Now, superstitious gal that I am, if I were running a cigarette theft ring and got a reading like that, I would have made some different decisions. But that's me. This story illustrates how we create our own karma by making good or bad choices. One of the interpretations of Justice is just that: Be mindful of your decisions at this time. Weigh your options with care. Above all, do the right thing, even if it's not the easy path.

Other ways of looking at this card: fairness, decisions, integrity, settling debts (karmic or otherwise), weighing the pros and cons, legal issues, making laws, and doing time.

Reversed, this card can indicate an injustice. Perhaps you got a raw deal. Maybe someone did you wrong. Whatever the case, you might be facing a sentence that seems unfair. It's also a sign of illegal activities. If you're up to no good and this card comes up, beware! Time to turn it around before the hammer comes down. Depending on the question and other cards involved (for example, Seven of Swords), the reversed Justice card can suggest that someone is getting away with a crime. This reversal can also warn of poor decision-making. If you're trying to decide between two courses of action, wait it out.

How to embody the energy of this card: Justice is a card that you can incorporate every single day of your life. Here's how: Just do the right thing. Period. Simple? On the surface, it's not because sometimes the right thing isn't black or white. The way to find the ethical path begins with mindfulness. Before making a decision or opening your mouth, stop. Take a moment to ask yourself, "How might my words or actions affect my life or the lives of others?" Marinate on that. Then, go forth and be a good human.

A question to ponder: *How do you act when you see injustice?*

Tarotcise

 Pull out the Magician, Hierophant, Devil, and Justice. Notice something? Every single one of them has one hand with a tool raised toward the sky and one pointing down to the earth. They may be holding different devices, but the message is the same: as above, so below. Reflect on what each card could be manifesting. Journal your findings.

THE HANGED MAN.

The Hanged Man

Card Number 12

NEPTUNE

The Hanged Man is another card that is often misunderstood. People assume it means something terrible, such as execution. But if you look at this card, you won't see a sign of struggle or any bloodshed. Instead, you'll notice a figure that seems to be hanging loose, a look of peace upon his face and a golden halo around his crown. This image certainly doesn't convey fear, does it? Instead, the vibe here is about surrender.

The image of a man hanging by one foot is called *pittura infamante*, which is Italian for "defaming portrait." These paintings were commonplace in Renaissance Italy and meant to shame thieves, traitors, and other sorts of criminals when no other legal recourse was available. They've also been used to mock the upper class when they've been caught in a crime. The Hanged Man is thought to be based on the *pittura infamante*.

In a tarot reading, the Hanged Man represents a sacrifice of sorts. Something must be given up to achieve a goal. This card says: get ready to go out on a limb to make something happen. If you've ever needed to do something without any gain, you've felt the energy of the Hanged Man.

It's also symbolic of letting go. Rather than struggle against events, accept them. Chill. Trust that all is going as it needs to. This means: have faith. Everything will work out as need be.

The Hanged Man can also indicate being yourself. This card favors going your own way rather than conforming to what everyone else is doing, even if that means being an outsider. Another popular interpretation is waiting things out. Things may not be ready to move at this time. All you can do is hang loose and bide your time. By taking a relaxed attitude, you may gain an entirely new perspective.

In some cases, this card can indeed indicate a traitor. Or, if it follows the Justice card in a question about a court case, it can symbolize a sentence being imposed. Due to the "wait" energy around this, I usually interpret this as jail time in those cases.

Other ways of looking at this card: release, a new perspective, hands are tied, left hanging, forgiveness, the martyr, relinquishing control, and suspension.

When the Hanged Man is reversed, it can indicate an inability to find freedom. Here, the figure is stuck up in the tree and cannot get down. This position can be interpreted as a hang-up—not just getting hung up due to circumstances, but also perhaps having an emotional hang-up such as holding on to an ex and refusing to move on.

This reversal could also be interpreted as an inability to be yourself. It's uptight and fearful. Instead of the trusting vibe of the right-side-up version of this card, the figure is unable to let go of anxiety or what others think. He becomes a prisoner in his own thoughts, unable to freely operate in the world.

In some cases, the Hanged Man reversed can symbolize a period when you have the ability to land on your feet . . . or get back on them after a severe trial. It can also represent a person who continually gripes about all they do for others. The guilt-tripping mother is an example of the Hanged Man reversed.

How to embody the energy of this card: Find the most tedious task you can—one that involves waiting. Standing in line at the Department of Motor Vehicles? Perfect! Now do your best to be completely calm. No matter what happens around you or how slowly the line moves, be as peaceful as can be, trusting that you'll eventually get up to the counter. Easy? Nope. Put anyone in a long line, and you'll rarely see people wearing their halos.

A question to ponder: *What is worth waiting for?*

Tarotcise

Notice that the Hanged Man's legs form the number four. Pull out all of the cards in the deck that have the number four or some variant (for example, Death is 13: 1 + 3 reduces down to 4.) What common themes do you find here? For example, the Hanged Man symbolizes the ability to let go completely. What might the Four of Swords have to say about faith? Look for the clues. Journal your findings.

Death

Card Number 13

SCORPIO

"**I** sure hope the Death card doesn't come up in my reading!" This is something every tarot reader will hear at one time or another. Popular media might be to blame for this; there are more than a few movies that portray the stereotype of the fortune-teller who pulls the Death card out, widens her eyes dramatically, and exclaims, "You're in grave danger!" This has given the Death card quite a stigma. (Did you ever notice the hero never dies despite these predictions? Hmmm . . .)

Here's the thing you need to know: the Death card doesn't mean physical death. It means something significant is about to come to an end to clear the way for a new beginning. In other words, this card indicates transformation.

Predicting actual death in a tarot reading is challenging, and many tarot readers won't even touch it for ethical reasons. Often, it doesn't show up with "scary" cards at all. People assume that you must see those fearful images to show the end of life, but actually, on the rare occasions that physical death does come in a tarot reading, it's usually much different from what the movies might lead you to believe. Our culture has a phobia about death, which is why we assume it must be negative. In tarot, it's a different story.

Speaking of stories, this one might illustrate the point well. A few years ago, my daughter and I were on a plane to San Francisco to celebrate her college graduation. School had been a long, hard slog for her, so it was time to blow off steam and eat like queens in one of our favorite cities. After two hours on the plane, we were bored, so I dug my tarot cards out of my bag to pass the time.

My daughter slowly shuffled the cards, focusing intently on her question. It was apparent this was a critical query, and she wanted to make sure that the cards were fully seasoned. She cut the deck and handed it to me and asked this: "Will I be financially independent this year? I'm sick of depending on Dad." At this time in her life, her father had been supporting her, and they often had furious rows, because every nickel he gave her had a string attached to it. This situation created a lot of friction in her life, and she was eager to put this behind her so that she could be self-sufficient . . . and get along better with him.

I laid out the cards, and they were fabulous. The Sun, Ten of Pentacles, Temperance. Great cards like that. Because the Sun is my go-to best card in the deck, I assumed this meant a bright future and a job. "Your future looks great here. It seems you will be completely independent before summer is over!" We started talking about possible employment and plans as I put the deck away.

A few weeks later, her father died of a sudden heart attack. She inherited a tidy sum of money and was on her own. This is how death shows up in a reading.

Another story! A client came to me in tears. Her husband had had an affair, and although they'd reconciled, she didn't feel secure in the relationship. They were still bickering, and she had tremendous fears that he would leave again. I pulled the Eight of Cups. "It looks like he's leaving again. Maybe permanently." She wasn't happy with the reading, and I didn't expect to hear from her again. (When you don't tell people what they want to hear, they often move on.) Lo and behold, I got a call. "Theresa, when you said he was going to leave me, could that mean death? Because he died in his sleep a few days ago."

Again, death rarely comes up in a reading, and these examples show that it may not be what you expect.

Now—let's dig into the Death card!

Like I mentioned before, Death indicates a change. Even if you are nervous about what's ahead, this card says: Embrace it. Move on. Put the past in the rearview mirror and look to the future. This is the card you want to see when you're thinking about making a significant life change. It's a call to relinquish the old, the outworn, or the things you've outgrown to make way for a new beginning.

Other ways of looking at this card: elimination, the unknown, conclusion, a call to simplify, cutting out the unnecessary, accepting your fate, and a vital ending.

The reversed meaning of this card amplifies the fear factor. That fear may lead to resistance or laziness. Instead of embracing the possibilities, the person becomes stubborn, digging in their heels, and refusing to let go. Hanging on for dear life is one of my favorite interpretations of this reversal. Even if the change is positive, someone who is unwilling to yield will cling to the past. Because sometimes, even a crappy history is more comforting than the fear of what might come. Those people who lament about the future and long for the "good ol' days"—which weren't so good—are an example of Death reversed.

How to embody the energy of this card: The best way to experience this card is by getting rid of something that no longer fits. That could be an old pair of pants you've been holding on to in the hopes you'd fit into a size 4 again, or it may be changing up your exercise routine because it's not producing any results. Look around you. What's old, stale, and not aligned with the life you want to live? Get rid of it. Then don't look back.

A question to ponder: *What needs to go?*

Tarotcise

 In this card are five figures: the skeleton figure on the horse, the dead king, the pope, the maiden, and the child. Notice how they are interacting (or not). What clues might those interactions give you? What are these figures saying to each other? What can you glean about their relationships . . . and their relationship to death? Journal your findings.

Temperance

Card Number 14

SAGITTARIUS

After the Death card, we move on to the calm vibe of the Temperance card. The angelic figure deftly pours a stream of water from one cup to another. Behind them, a gold crown rises above a path. This card symbolizes peace, balance, and healing. When this card turns up in a tarot reading, it's a sign that you're able to come to terms with past events and perhaps you've learned something valuable. Those experiences can lead to making better, conscious choices in the future.

As a card of balance, Temperance favors the middle way. Instead of extremes, this card says: Find the center. That's the sweet spot. When you operate from that place, you're no longer being dictated to by your reactions or desires. Instead, you're finding your flow and moving through the world with grace.

Notice how the figure gingerly puts one toe into the water while the other remains firmly planted on the earth. This could mean testing the waters to see if something is a go . . . or not. Experimenting before making a firm decision means you're doing your due diligence. Or this could be interpreted as bringing different elements together and finding harmony between the two. For example, a happy blended family would be Temperance in action.

Sometimes this card advises patience. Don't rush to make a decision. Sit with it. Weigh all of your options.

I've also seen this card come up when someone is healing from illness. It's a sign that the body is working hard to come back into balance.

Other ways of looking at this card: alchemy, abstaining, a sensible approach, blending, stillness, biding your time, tolerance, refinement, and a "happy medium."

The reversed Temperance is unbalanced energy. Instead of calm, this becomes disruptive, unstable. The figure loses his footing and stumbles. Things go to extremes. Those extremes could be habits such as overeating or overindulging in drugs or alcohol. But they can also be an inability to control a situation. The center is lost and chaos reigns. Peace is replaced with anarchy. If this reversal shows up with the Devil, it's a warning that habits are leading you down a dark place.

Other interpretations of Temperance reversed are indecision and impatience. Can't make up your mind and you're driving everyone else nuts? Bingo.

How to embody the energy of this card: One of the best ways to integrate this card is through the Vrksasana, or tree, yoga pose. Finding your center in this pose takes practice, but once you master it, you'll feel a sense of tranquility washing over you. Here's how to do the pose. Stand up nice and straight. Pour all of your energy into your left leg. Envision it as sturdy as a tree trunk. Take your right foot and bring it up to rest on your calf or thigh. Engage your abdominals and lengthen your torso. Visualize the crown of your head reaching to the sky. Bring both hands in prayer position in front of your heart. Take a few deep breaths, and if you feel called, lift your hands above your head and separate your fingers as if you are growing branches. Take a few more breaths and relax into the pose. You may feel a bit shaky. Be patient. Breathe into it. Stay grounded for a minute or so. Then slowly lower your hands back to your heart and release your right foot. Repeat on the other side. Notice how centered— or not—you feel when you hold this pose. Were you able to find balance?

A question to ponder: *When life throws you a curveball, how do you react?*

Tarotcise

 Find all the cards with two cups or vessels in the deck. How are each of the figures handling those cups? Cups symbolize emotions. What emotions might be at play in each of these cards?

The Devil

Card Number 15

CAPRICORN

The Devil is another one of those tarot cards that strikes fear into people. Take a peek, and you'll see a mean-looking demon with two naked people chained to him. This imagery is probably the reason many people assume that the tarot cards are evil. (Psst, they are not. They are a tool made out of seventy-eight paper cards. Nothing evil about 'em unless you have questionable motives for using them.)

The Devil symbolizes bondage, as in getting yourself into a dark place. You're trapped—for example, an addiction to drugs or alcohol. Or becoming a slave to some other desire. It can also indicate negativity and misery. Moreover, materialism.

However you slice it, this is not a happy card to see. When it shows up in a reading, it's a signal that you need to examine how you've gotten yourself into the current circumstance. Look closely, and you'll notice that the figures are wearing loose chains. This says that you may have gotten yourself into a dill pickle, but you can get out. To stay or go—it's up to you to take personal responsibility. No using the "devil made me do it" as a cop-out. In some cases, this card can indicate accepting your bad situation. Think of the person who stays in a terrible relationship because of money or the fear of not being able to find anything better.

Sometimes, this card can indicate control. Instead of being the victim, you've taken on the devil role and are now the oppressor. I've seen this come up for bosses who were ruling over their employees with a heavy metal fist. In a romantic relationship, this control can be a jealous spouse who is constantly blowing up their partner's phone with "Where are you?" texts and worse.

In a question about choices, this card can say: you need to choose between the devil you know and the devil you don't.

Other ways of looking at this card: ignorance, obsession, giving up your independence, submission, a dark cloud, absence of light, hopelessness, negativity, ego-driven desires, wounding, lust, and shadow work.

The reversal indicates a total release. Liberation time! Instead of being stuck in a jam, you're free to go. This could be moving away from a situation that comes to an end or finding the courage to give up your addictions and face your demons. You're back in control of your life. The Devil reversed can also indicate the rejection of materialism. Get back to the simpler things. Do you really need that rare ostrich Birkin bag? *Nope.*

How to embody the energy of this card: A fun way to incorporate the power of the Devil is by doing something naughty. Eat the cupcake, pull a prank on a loved one, play hooky. Be a little bad. Not too bad though, m'kay?

A question to ponder: *What makes you feel trapped?*

Tarotcise

 Grab the Lovers and the Devil. Once again, like in our previous Tarotcise for the Lovers, ponder the figures in these cards. How are the characters in the Lovers similar to the Devil? (Hint: there is an element here of temptation. Look closely.) What do the flames in both cards suggest? What themes here about choices and release might you find in each card? Journal your answers.

The Tower

Card Number 16

MARS

Crash bang boom! That's the vibe of the Tower card! All you need to do is see those figures leaping out of the inferno, and you know that the Tower isn't messing around. This card symbolizes chaos, a major upheaval, or unexpected change that rocks the foundation to the core.

The Tower is another one of those cards that make people groan when they see it. The image is certainly not subtle, and neither are the interpretations. The Tower can represent a situation that goes through a massive shake-up, like a revolution or the overthrow of an established structure. In relationships, this is the violent breakup where there is no turning back. What once stood firm now burns to the ground, leaving nothing in its wake but ashes. Destructive? Yes. But know this: that wreckage needs to happen. Whatever is being torn down was built on a flimsy foundation, and this upheaval, while frightening, is necessary so that something better can be made in its place.

There is another side to this card: liberation. Although the figures seem to be freaking out, they are getting free of an oppressive situation. Even freedom can feel off-putting to those who have grown accustomed to the "way things are." The Tower promises to bring a chance for a fresh start, but first, we must be ready to liberate ourselves . . . or be freed from other circumstances.

One of the interpretations I love for this card is the wake-up call. That lightning bolt strikes the tower, but if you notice, a crown is flying off the top. I see that as the crown chakra getting blown wide open! Think of a time when you got that sudden bolt of inspiration that made you sit up and take notice. That might have been a genius idea or a message from the Universe that spurs you to make a change finally. Either way, those jolts to the brain can be a good thing—the motivation that creates a crucial life shift.

The other energy here is that of a storm that comes and clears the air. That argument with your mother-in-law that allows you to set boundaries? That's an example of the Tower in action.

Other ways of looking at this card: being humbled, a surprise, a meltdown, the fall from grace, purging, initiation, an economic crash, and the collapse of a government.

The reversal still suggests significant changes, but instead of a massive blowout, the vibe is softer, less intense. I've seen this card come up when people are getting prepared for a change, such as news at work that may indicate a new CEO coming in. Instead of a shock to the system, the Tower reversed says: you have time to adapt. It can also be seen as softening the blow. The old "it's not you, it's me" speech to that partner you just aren't feeling? Tower reversed.

The other way of looking at this reversal is the fear of change. Instead of taking the leap, you remain in that burning tower, hoping that you're going to get saved . . . or that the storm will pass. Like the Devil card, the Tower reversed shows you're choosing to remain in place, even if the situation isn't for your highest good.

How to embody the energy of this card: The Tower is a card of drastic energy. So how can you incorporate this without doing something crazy like jumping out of a building? There are other risks you can take that might be less dangerous. Risks such as finally telling that person how you feel. Or signing up for that class you've been too scared to join. Saying no to that request that feels like a drag or saying yes to that job offer that means you're going to have to step up your game—both Tower energies. Do something that feels like a mighty scary risk today . . . but stay safe!

A question to ponder: *What needs to go, right now?*

Tarotcise

Get out the Devil card and the Tower. Notice how they are both the same when you reverse 'em? The Devil reversed is the Tower, and the Tower reversed is the Devil. What other cards in the deck might complement each other in this way? Go through your deck and dig them out!

The Star

Card Number 17

AQUARIUS

THE STAR.

Ah, the Star. After the Devil and the Tower, this card is a welcome relief. The image on the card is peaceful, chill. A beautiful figure gently pours water from two vessels as she gazes into the pond. Stars twinkle in the background as a bird watches from a tree in the distance. It's the calm after the storm, the balm that brings healing, and inspiration for the future. This is hope in a card, friends. When it shows up in a tarot reading, the Star says, "It's going to be alright." The crisis is over, and now the task of rebuilding is here. But it's not daunting like the Ten of Wands. Instead, the energy here is hopeful.

This card represents the power of belief and positivity, which keeps us going, no matter what has happened. It's also one of the "wish" cards in the tarot deck. If you are focusing on a specific goal and this card turns up, your wish will be granted.

The Star is one of the best cards to see if you are healing from an illness or surgery. It's also a goody if you're looking to get famous. A star is born!

Other ways of looking at this card: inspiration, balance, pouring your heart and soul into a situation, the light at the end of the tunnel, getting your groove back, and finding your center.

When the Star card is reversed, the hope is gone. Instead, the Star turns pensive and pessimistic. What you want is out of reach or delayed. Or perhaps your mindset is not allowing good to come into your world at this time. The Star reversed can symbolize depression or illness. It's a sign that something has become stagnant, and healing is needed. An adjustment is necessary—either with your attitude or lifestyle. This card can also indicate that creative channels are blocked; instead of being able to express yourself freely, you're inhibited in some way.

How to embody the energy of this card: This is the card of positive thinking. A great practice that will help you feel the power of this card is to try not to complain for thirty days. Sounds easy? It's not! But it will change your world, I promise. Pick a date and start. If you find yourself complaining, start all over again at day one. Once you've gotten through the thirty days, you'll be surprised at how great you feel. Positive. Grateful. Like a total Star!

A question to ponder: *How can hope thrive even in dark times?*

Tarotcise

 Pretend that you're a reporter and your job is to interview the figure in this card. What questions would you ask her? (For example, "Why are you naked?") What answers might she give you? Get inside her head and see what she might have to say to you. Journal your answers.

The Moon

Card Number 18

PISCES

THE MOON.

The Moon card shows two canines howling at the moon while a little lobster hesitates at the water's edge. No doubt he's unsure what those dogs are up to, so he holds back and waits.

This image sums up the energy of this card, which is fear, uncertainty, and an inability to see clearly. This Moon is about things that go bump in the night, the dark night of the soul, and illusions. Hence, it's a card that often produces anxiety when it comes up in a tarot reading. That's because not knowing what's ahead can be frightening. Why? People don't like it when they are not in control of things.

The Moon shows that things are not what they seem to be, and changes may be happening. Because of the lack of clarity, this card advises pausing and reflecting, just like that little lobster guy. You'll need to kick back or let your instincts guide you. It can also indicate danger is ahead, but if you allow your intuition to lead the way, you should be able to avoid trouble. Like the High Priestess, this card can indicate the awakening of the intuitive faculties. If you've been ignoring those hunches, the Moon may be saying, "Hey, pay attention; this is hella important."

Other ways of looking at this card: imagination, shadow work, confusion, lunatics, deception, lack of direction, lost, the unfamiliar, and lucid dreaming.

When the Moon card is reversed, it's a sign that things are finally clear. You're getting the go-ahead on that plan, or a detour is out of the way, which means you can proceed with confidence. The Moon reversed could also be interpreted as "seeing the light" or a wake-up call that allows you to know what your next step should be. In some situations, this card can still indicate fear, particularly if the emotions and imagination are running wild. Then the Moon becomes an emotional crisis or lunacy. The animal nature takes over.

How to embody the energy of this card: Because this is the card of fear, one of the best ways to feel the power is to watch a scary movie. Pick one that has that feeling of "something happening in the dark." *Halloween* is perfect! Now turn off all the lights. See if you can find a way to be comfortable with discomfort. Boo!

A question to ponder: *Have you ever experienced a dark night of the soul?*

Tarotcise

 Pull out all the cards that have moons in them. What role does each moon play in the various cards? Are they fearful or not? What might the presence of the moon in each card suggest about the other figures?

The Sun

Card Number 19

SUN

THE SUN .

One look at the Sun card and you know something good is on the way. The radiant child with arms outstretched riding on a horse and the sun lighting up the sky—this card says: happy days are here again! The Sun is the card you want to see in your reading, for it indicates everything is becoming positive and joyful. Abundance and success vibrate strongly. This is a rebirth, beauty, wonder, and the promise of a new day.

The Sun is a fantastic card for anything around children as well or for being a kid at heart.

Other ways of looking at this card: fame, epiphanies, glory, radiance, good health, vitality, confidence, enlightenment, illumination, courage, and prosperity.

When the Sun is reversed, it's still a happy card, but the energy is a bit dim. Think of this as a cloudy day when there is potential for good . . . or a storm. Suddenly, things aren't so bright. Outside influences may be affecting the situation, or perhaps you've just lost your way a bit. It's also possible you're bringing the dark cloud yourself. If you're having trouble finding the joy in a situation, you can be channeling the energy of the Sun reversed. I call this the "Eeyore" card, for the donkey from *Winnie the Pooh* who always seems to find the gloom 'n doom side of things no matter how bright it really is. The Sun reversed can also indicate joy delayed or a situation that cannot come to full fruition. Sometimes, this reversal can signal a need to heal or free the inner child. Let them come out to play!

How to embody the energy of this card: Spend a day doing something that brings you childlike joy. Fly a kite, hike in the woods, play a board game, hit the playground. Better yet, bring a child with you! Enjoy an entire day devoted to kid-centered activities. Have fun!

A question to ponder: *When have you felt completely silly?*

Tarotcise

 Get ready for some creative play! Using the Sun card as a prompt, create a fairy tale for a child. What might the figures be doing? What lessons might they encounter along the way? How might the Sun's themes of positivity and joy be part of the moral to the story? Have fun with this! Bonus: read it to a child.

Judgement

Card Number 20

PLUTO

JUDGEMENT.

Judgement is the card of rebirth. On this card in the Rider-Waite-Smith deck, people are rising from their graves, arms outstretched toward an angel in the sky, blaring a horn. This signals the end of the old life and the beginning of the new. It's time to put the past behind you and instead rise up to embrace the possibilities! Life can begin anew. Shed that old skin. The former you is dead and gone. The past is firmly in the past.

Judgement can also symbolize the wake-up call, or epiphany, that spurs you into making a major about-face. It can also be the higher calling, the life's work, or a reckoning. Whether it's a call to evolve or to step into your power, when this card shows up in a tarot reading, you must heed the call.

In some cases, Judgement can say: Trust your own judgement here. Make your own call!

Other ways of looking at this card: rebirth, renewal, judging a situation, being judged, asking for mercy, seeing things in a whole new way, atonement, forgiveness, and salvation.

Judgement reversed indicates that at some level, you're refusing to hear the call. Perhaps you're like an ostrich with your head in the sand, unwilling to see the signs. Or you may see them but are too stubborn to make the change. So you cling to what's old and familiar, even if it sucks.

Sometimes this reversal can indicate that you hear the call, but you just don't know what to do about it. This may be due to fear, or perhaps you've convinced yourself that you can't do it. This means you may be making excuses. Like the drug addict who gets an opportunity to enter rehab but then starts some song and dance about needing to "take care of some business first . . . ." That is Judgement reversed. The possibility of change is there, but instead of going for it, you remain firmly in the grave.

One other thing that this reversal can indicate: terrible judgement. Think of a time when you got a bad vibe but went ahead and did something anyway.

How to embody the energy of this card: Because this card is all about renewal, do something to rejuvenate yourself. Sit in a sauna or get a massage. Detoxify your system with a cleansing diet. Give up sugar for a month. Try those sorts of things. Notice how much better your body feels when you take good care of it.

A question to ponder: *What makes you feel reborn?*

Tarotcise

 The cross in the angel's flag on this card symbolizes the four elements or four directions. Think about the four elements in the Minor Arcana: Earth, Air, Fire, Water. What direction might each of those elements point to? For example, if you were called to follow the Earth element, what might that mean? If the Universe is nudging you to go in a Water direction, what might be the advice given? Take your time to explore orientation and the elements.

The World

Card Number 21

SATURN

With the World, we reach the final card in the Major Arcana series. It symbolizes the end. A goal has been successfully achieved. Bravo! The World says, "You've made it!" Time to celebrate your success. All that work you've been doing pays off at long last. This is the graduation ceremony before the next level. A chapter closes at last. Take a moment to collect your reward and then get ready . . . there is a new journey ahead. One cycle closes, and another is on the way.

Other ways of looking at this card: wholeness, integration, world travel, distance, fame, visibility, inclusiveness, worldly success, and closure.

When you reverse this card, it's like your world is being turned upside down. Instead of reaching a conclusion, you're back to square one . . . or in limbo. Nothing is moving ahead, and closure is impossible. The energy of this reversal is one of stagnation. There is a sense of being incomplete, and that can only change when you're ready to take responsibility and free yourself. Remember: even if you decide to remain in place, the world still turns.

How to embody the energy of this card: Find a reason to celebrate an achievement. You don't have to do anything elaborate, nor does this need to be a significant milestone. Just something important to you. Perhaps it might be that final cigarette. Or getting that A on your history exam. Or maybe your commitment to your tarot studies and that moment when you finally grasp the meaning of the Death card. Choose something and then create a little celebration ceremony. Light a candle, eat a cupcake, or raise a glass in a toast. Huzzah!

A question to ponder: *What achievement are you the proudest of at this time?*

Tarotcise

 In the tarot deck, many cards can symbolize an ending of sorts: not just the World but Death, the Tower, the Wheel of Fortune, and in the Minor Arcanas, you can look at the Eights, Nines, and Tens. Go through the deck and find them all. What similarities can you find? How might each depict an ending differently? How might you interpret a tarot reading with all "ending" cards? Journal your thoughts.

• • •

We've completed our exploration of the Major Arcana. Take a minute to catch your breath. Grab some tea and get comfortable. We're going to run through the Minor Arcana next. Ready? Let's do this!

The Minor Arcana

To recap: the fifty-six Minor Arcana cards deal with the day-to-day events and people interacting with you. These are the things you can control on some level. Each suit is associated with a different element of human concern:

• Wands
Passion, employment, creativity, physical energy, building

• Cups
Feelings, emotions, relationships, love, connection

• Swords
Conflicts, thoughts, intellect, mental force

• Pentacles
Material goods, security, money, values

ACE of WANDS.

The Ace of Wands

Element: Fire

The Ace of Wands symbolizes a new creative venture, a fresh start, and an olive branch being offered. This is the chance to turn over a new leaf . . . or to begin that new job finally! Aces indicate a new beginning, and in the fiery Wands element, the Ace is the beginning of a passion. Whether this is a creative project or a hot new affair, this card says: go for it!

This card is also what I call my "yes" or "thumbs-up" card in the tarot deck. It's my affirmative when asking a yes or no question.

The Ace of Wands is often associated with the birth of a child. That birth doesn't always need to come in a human form either; it can be anything you're creating.

Other ways of looking at this card: confidence, excitement, the spark, the power needed to get something off the ground, a new enterprise, opportunity.

The reversed Ace of Wands is like a car that ran out of gas. The energy may start off with lots of promise, but suddenly it stops in its tracks. The fire goes out. Sometimes this could be due to circumstances like having poor timing or from trying to force something before it's ready. Whatever the case, the situation turns cold or descends into chaos. This can also symbolize an opportunity that gets snatched away. That promotion you thought you were getting that got passed over to the boss's son? A perfect example. This reversal can also indicate a passion that dies. For example, a relationship that loses its spark. If no one is willing to keep the fire burning, there is little chance that it can continue.

How to embody the energy of this card: Start a new artistic project. That might be picking up a brush and canvas to begin working on your first masterpiece or perhaps finally deciding to paint that ugly bedroom a beautiful shade of blue. Find a project that excites you and go for it!

A question to ponder: *What does it mean to live passionately?*

Tarotcise

 Gather the Aces. Lay them side by side in pairs. Aces can symbolize an offering. Let's say the Ace of Pentacles and Ace of Cups are facing each other. What are these two cards offering each other? How might they respond to each other? How about the Ace of Pentacles with the Ace of Wands? Move them around. What if you put the Ace of Swords next to the Ace of Pentacles? Now they aren't facing each other, but they are looking in the same direction. What might that hint at? How about if you put the Ace of Cups next to the Ace of Swords? In this position, they are back to back. What clues might that give you about the energy between these Aces? Journal your findings.

The Two of Wands

Element: Fire

On the Two of Wands, a figure stands in a fortress with a globe in his hand, looking out at the ocean. One thing is for sure: he's in a good position. That's what this card says when it comes up in a tarot reading. Plans are coming together, and success is assured. You may have achieved a cherished goal, and now you're gearing up for the next big thing. Ahead, there is much planning that needs to be done. Explore your options and set goals.

Twos can also symbolize options and choices. The Two of Wands says: the possibilities are limitless. The world is in your hands. You can go as big as you want and in any direction you desire.

Other ways of looking at this card: respect, security, gaining power, courage, strategy, and everybody wants to rule the world.

When this card is reversed, the planning is at an end and action is advised. No more sitting back and plotting. This card says: let's get this show on the road! Take a risk and get out of your comfort zone. Outside is a big world waiting for your arrival. He who hesitates loses. The only way to win is to take action, even if you're not entirely sure of your goal. This could also indicate a time when you're being passive or playing it too safe. In some cases, it's a lack of foresight.

How to embody the energy of this card: Because this card is about success and planning, a fun way to "be" this card is to plan a trip to somewhere far. Even if you don't have the desire actually to go anywhere, use your imagination! Research interesting places. Look at what actually getting there might entail for you. Would you travel by air or sea? What sights might you see? Who would go with you? Plot out a big adventure. Extra credit: go.

A question to ponder: *What would your life look like if all your plans worked out the way you wanted?*

Tarotcise

 If you were the figure in this card, where might you be facing? As you can see, he's looking out at a body of water. Which one? Is he viewing the Atlantic Ocean or the Great Lakes? How might different locations affect his point of view or his plans? Let your imagination lead the way and journal your findings.

The Three of Wands

Element: Fire

Like the Two of Wands, in the Three of Wands, we see a figure looking out at an ocean. But this guy isn't sitting in the fortress making plans. He's gearing up for a journey . . . or waiting for his ship to come to shore. This image symbolizes being out in the world, ready for the next big step. New adventures are on the horizon! You have much to look forward to. Sure, you've already accomplished a lot, but why rest on your laurels? This card says: expand. There's more out there for you. This is also one of my favorite cards to see in a question about travel.

Other ways of looking at this card: boldness, exploration, looking ahead, excitement, adventure, visionary, world domination, quest, leadership, and conquest.

The reversed Three of Wands indicates that plans are not working out. A total flop. What you hoped for isn't possible. It's time to go back to the drawing board and revise. Scrutinize your goals. Do they make sense? Or are you embarking on an impossible dream? In a question about travel, this is not the card you want to see, because it means that the trip isn't happening. Everything is on hold.

How to embody the energy of this card: Stop looking to the past. Instead, start thinking about your future. What's the next big thing you'd like to do? What's calling you? What do you want to welcome into your life? Dream about the possibilities and then create your bucket list!

A question to ponder: *What's next?*

Tarotcise

Pay attention to the hand gestures in the Wands suit. Look at the forceful grip of the Ace of Wands versus the way this figure holds on to his wand. Notice the difference? He seems to be leaning on it for support. What about the rest of the Wands suit? Note how each figure holds the wand. What does this tell you about the energy of the card?

The Four of Wands

Element: Fire

The Four of Wands is one of the cards I love to see in a reading because it symbolizes good times and celebrations. The party scene tells you: it's time to kick off your shoes and dance up a storm! Like the figures in this card, be joyful. Give thanks for how far you've come or how much you have. Enjoy the rewards you've earned. This card promises the touchdown, the crossing of the finish line, the successful completion of a goal. The celebration scene can also be just that: a ceremony or joyful event such as a homecoming, wedding, or family reunion. Optimism and joy are in the air. Things are looking up!

Other ways of looking at this card: freedom, triumph, cutting loose, concerts, and the welcoming committee.

Even when you reverse this card, the joy remains. It may be less boisterous, but it's a celebration nonetheless. Or perhaps there are reasons to be grateful, but they're not apparent. Look around you—you may find that you've got plenty of reasons to be happy.

How to embody the energy of this card: Throw a party! Send out invitations. Get the house cleaned. Set out some nibbles and open the wine. Gather your friends and family. You don't need a reason to have a get-together. Just an excuse to be in each other's company, enjoying time together, is enough. Remember: you can make any moment special.

A question to ponder: *What can you celebrate right now?*

Tarotcise

 Pull the Tower card out of the deck. You'll notice that the figures in the Tower and the Four of Wands are dressed the same. If you put these cards side by side, you can see a story emerging. Try it with the Tower first followed by the Four of Wands. This could indicate a miraculous escape. What about if you reverse the cards? What might the story be then?

The Five of Wands

Element: Fire

In the Five of Wands, the figures seem to be in some sort of battle. Or is it a game? Whatever they're doing, the spirit of competition is present. This might be a power play or a competitive sport. It's not harmful either. Instead, the vibe here is friendly. Maybe exciting. Although it looks like a fight on the outside, there is playfulness here. Sometimes you need a challenge to grow. The Five of Wands says: bring it on! This is good to see if you're looking to shake things up at work. Ready to lay down some new rules? This card indicates the time to do so is now.

At times, depending on the other cards involved, this card can indicate a negative competition. For example, if this card were hanging out with the Devil, we might see a rival stepping in between you and your partner!

Other ways of looking at this card: opponents, the thrill of the chase, setbacks, interference, irritation, distractions, a lack of leadership, or too many cooks in the kitchen.

The reversed Five of Wands takes some of the fun out of the competition. Instead of being exhilarating, it becomes a blood sport. The rules are tossed out, and it's a free-for-all. I often see this as dirty politics or playing dirty. The political campaign where one party slanders the other is a perfect example of the Five of Wands reversed. Darwinism is taken to the extreme. This reversal can also symbolize giving up. Instead of going for it, you're intimidated by the competition, so you just put down your stick and walk away.

How to embody the energy of this card: Get involved in a competitive sport, but make it fun! A great idea would be gathering a few of your friends and engaging in some Frisbee golf. It's easy yet challenging . . . and a whole lotta horseplay! Plus, it's an excellent excuse to hang with your buddies and blow off some steam. May the best person win! (Psst, remember, it's not about the win—it's the thrill of the game.)

A question to ponder: *What makes you feel competitive?*

Tarotcise

Take out the Five of Wands and the Five of Swords. Both cards depict battle scenes. What sorts of fighting might you find in each card? How are they different? How are they the same? Look through the deck to locate the other cards with battle scenes (yes, there are more). What modern-day battles might these cards depict?

The Six of Wands

Element: Fire

After the battle, the victory parade! The Six of Wands shows the champion surrounded by a cheering crowd. Huzzah! A great triumph has been achieved, and now you're stepping into the winner's circle. The destination has not yet been reached, but you're well on your way. The vibe here is one of optimism. You're seeing the road ahead, and it's looking bright and open. Mission accomplished. Or is it? Keep on moving along. Soon enough, you'll know the outcome. This card is as confident as it gets. With a few wins under your belt, you would be feeling on top of your game too.

Other ways of looking at this card: getting back in the saddle, pride, leadership, pursuing the dream, fame, supporting the winning team, we are the champions.

But what about when the Six of Wands is reversed? Here, the figure is unable to get in the saddle. Instead, he falters and leads his team astray. This is the card of poor leadership as well as defeat. The goal cannot be completed. There is more work yet to be done. The Six of Wands reversed can also symbolize a lack of support. If you cannot rally your team, reaching victory may be hard.

In some cases, this reversal can also symbolize a fall from grace. A coup d'état. Or perhaps the realization that the emperor has no clothes. You're forced to come down off your high horse. Public humiliation.

How to embody the energy of this card: Think of a time when you needed the support of others to reach a goal. Having that team cheering you on probably felt pretty good, right? Try to embody that by finding someone else to support. This person could be a loved one going back to school or a colleague completing a marathon. It doesn't matter who or what the end goal is. What matters is that you get behind them and encourage them until the finish line is crossed. Now, the flip side of that: the next time you're setting a goal, ask for support. Let others help you step up your game!

A question to ponder: *When does victory taste the sweetest for you?*

Tarotcise

 The number six is connected to harmony and the caretaker. How does that energy show up in the Six of Wands? Journal your findings.

The Seven of Wands

Element: Fire

After the sweet victory dance of the Six of Wands, we now see that the win was short-lived. The Seven of Wands is not resting on his laurels. Instead, he's encountering new challenges. No doubt some of these are aggravating, but the figure presses on. Such is life. You overcome one situation only to face three more down the road. The Seven of Wands represents new struggles. They must be met with the full force of your being. Pushing forward may be overwhelming, but you must continue. Another victory is possible or, at the very least, you'll be able to keep the wolves at bay with a valiant effort.

In some cases, this card can indicate a need to defend your turf. Hold your ground.

Other ways of looking at this card: aggression, opposition, force, boundaries, strength, going on the attack, and courage in the face of great adversity.

The reversed meaning of this card is giving up the fight. Maybe you're just too tired to continue. Or the forces aligned against you are too strong. Or perhaps you just don't give a damn. Whatever the case may be, you've become overpowered and now just need to put down your weapons and surrender. This card is the stinging defeat that happens when you are surrounded by all sides and cannot fight your way out. Admitting defeat and raising the white flag suck, but sometimes that's okay. When you can't keep it going, get going. Some battles are not worth fighting.

It's also possible that you didn't try hard enough. You didn't fight for the girl, and now some other schmuck has won her heart. Shoulda tried harder, pal.

How to embody the energy of this card: The Seven of Wands fights for what they believe in. One of the best ways to live this card is by getting involved in a good cause. That may be saving whales or fighting climate change. Find something that you're willing to fight for and then do it! Take a stand!

A question to ponder: *What is truly worth fighting for?*

Tarotcise

Take out the first seven Wands cards that we've covered so far. Lay them out in sequential order. If this were a storyboard for a movie, which one would it be? Why? Journal your thoughts. Extra credit! Write a plotline based on the Wands from cards Ace through Seven.

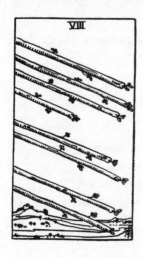

The Eight of Wands

Element: Fire

Unlike most of the Minors, the Eight of Wands has no human figures. Instead, eight wands are flying through the air. Who threw them? Why? Where are the rods going? It's hard to say, but one thing is clear: there is movement.

This is the card of swiftness and progress. No speed bumps are in the way, which means you can expect a lot of ground is going to be covered . . . quickly. The Eight of Wands symbolizes exciting news and acceleration. Everything is going according to plan. Maybe even better than thought. Full speed ahead!

Other ways of looking at this card: travel, passion, love notes, essential messages, a whirlwind romance, taking action, endings, efficiency, exploration, or a sudden resolution.

The Eight of Wands reversed doesn't necessarily stop the progress, but it sure does slow it down. This is like driving with one foot on the brake—stop 'n go all the way. Instead of the quick progress of the upright version, it's a long, hard slog. It may be that you don't have the gas to go or perhaps you just don't know where to direct your energy. Things slow to a crawl, and you may have to retrace your steps to see where you went wrong.

A few years ago, I was supposed to be heading across the pond to England for a tarot conference. That morning, I pulled the Eight of Wands reversed. I was a bit concerned, but thought, nah, everything looks fine. Bags were packed, not a cloud in the sky—everything should have been smooth as gravy. But as I sat waiting to board, an ominous dark cloud began to roll in out of nowhere, and it began to pour. Needless to say, the flight was canceled, and I was sent home. The next day, I came back to the airport. Same thing. On the third day, I boarded the plane only to sit on the tarmac for over an hour before the airline deplaned us and said there were weather problems. I never made it to England. Now when I travel, I take a deep breath and hope the Eight of Wands reversed does not make an appearance. So far, it hasn't happened, and I've made every other flight!

How to embody the energy of this card: Since the Eight of Wands is connected to movement, the best way to feel this card is by moving your body. Shake your groove thing on the dance floor or sign up for a half marathon and begin training. Ready, set, GO!

A question to ponder: *What needs to get moving?*

Tarotcise

 The Eight of Wands is one of the only cards without human figures. Go through the deck and find all the cards that have zero humans in them. Look at each one and ask yourself: if there were a human on this card, what actions might they be taking . . . or not? Journal your thoughts.

The Nine of Wands

Element: Fire

On the Nine of Wands, the figure stands, holding on warily to a wand, his head bandaged. His face seems uncertain, nervous, and full of dread. This is the setback, that situation that you thought was behind you, but uh-oh, it's baaacckkkk! Now you've got to hit reverse and finish what you've started. Ugh. But once it's done, you can move on.

The Nine of Wands can also indicate paranoia. An old betrayal that haunts you. That loss you never quite got over. The old wound that won't seem to heal no matter how hard you try. So you're overly suspicious of everything.

Other ways of looking at this card: taking a stand, perseverance despite the odds, assuming the worst, determination, boundaries, trust issues, finding the strength to push on, or not letting someone in.

When this card is reversed, it can say: Drop your guard. Let down your walls and be open. Instead of suspicion, find trust. This reversal can also indicate that a job is close to being finished. At long last, progress is ahead. You've overcome the problems and can now cruise toward victory.

How to embody the energy of this card: Find an unfinished project. This could be anything—painting that room, clearing out the garage, finishing that homework assignment, reading that book on the shelf. Pick a task that you've put on hold, go back, and get it done.

A question to ponder: *What wound still needs to heal?*

Tarotcise

Go through the tarot deck and find all the cards that show figures wearing bandages. What do these bandages symbolize? A wound? An inability to move or see? Journal your thoughts on the symbolism of bandages.

The Ten of Wands

Element: Fire

I'm a workaholic, so the Ten of Wands never bothers me. After all, it's the hardest-working card in the deck. The figure is bent over with a heavy load of wands, slowly trudging toward home. The bundle of rods signifies a burden, while the house shows a goal yet to be reached. This represents the significant effort needed to achieve your goal. I like to visualize the guy from the Nine of Wands, grabbing all those wands and putting his back into it.

When this card comes up in a reading, you're being called to take on major responsibilities. This is a time when you cannot shirk your duties. Instead, you must bust a move and trudge on, no matter how great the load may seem. Soon enough, you'll reach your goal. But until that day comes, as RuPaul says, "You better work."

Other ways of looking at this card: hard labor, oppression, taking on other people's problems, peer pressure, trying to do it all, overtime, pushing too hard, going it alone, tough times, the struggle is real.

When this card is reversed, the burden lifts. Things ease up or perhaps someone else helps to pull up the slack. Relief at last after a long, hard road. Whatever you've been working toward is finally reached or resolved.

How to embody the energy of this card: Pick a task that feels like a challenge. For me, that might be finishing this book! Now, put your head down and just do it. Keep going until the job is done. Commit! Another way to feel this card is by being a shoulder for someone else to lean on. Let someone unload their burdens on you. Be strong for them.

A question to ponder: *When have you taken one for the team?*

Tarotcise

Line up the Eight of Wands, Nine of Wands, and Ten of Wands. What story do these cards tell you? How does the good news of the Eight of Wands translate into all this hard work?

PAGE of WANDS.

The Page of Wands

Element: Fire

Pages symbolize messages, and this particular Page brings good news. This could be a new creative venture or job. It's the start of something awesome, so trust that when the Page of Wands shows up in a reading, he's bringing something positive.

But this Page can also symbolize a person. In that case, it's a youthful, energetic person who can be impulsive at times. They may have a passion they're pursuing, and whatever the interest may be, you can be sure the approach is enthusiastic. This can be the athlete on a scholarship or the super-nerd who is going for their academic goals with gusto. Remember—anyone can be a Page! Even an older person can play this role; all it requires is a passion that must be pursued.

Sometimes the Page of Wands indicates a new beginning. The Wands suit favors work or creativity, so the beginning may be a promotion, a new job, or the start of a new project. Any seeds planted now can grow.

Other ways of looking at this card: originality, confidence, inspiration, talent, independence, enthusiasm, and the spirit of adventure.

When this Page is reversed, the enthusiasm wanes. The interest dies, and you're off to the next new thing. In some cases, this could indicate unwelcome news. Or something that never quite gets off the ground. The reversed Page of Wands can also symbolize a rebellious youth or a slacker.

How to embody the energy of this card: Be on the lookout for good news today. This could be something personal . . . or something in the world. Whatever the story is, celebrate!

A question to ponder: *What seeds are you planting at this time, and how do you plan to grow them?*

Tarotcise

Both the Ace of Wands and Page of Wands symbolize a new job or creative venture. But how are these cards different in their expression of this message? How might they find common ground? What similarities do you notice between these cards? Journal your discoveries.

KNIGHT of WANDS.

The Knight of Wands

Element: Fire

This fiery fella is passion times ten! Whatever the Knight of Wands does and wherever he goes, you can be sure that he's bringing it—full on. That's because he's action-oriented. Instead of sitting on his desires, he goes for them. This character symbolizes bravado, courage, and the ability to take a risk. This card can also indicate sexual heat—that first flush of excitement of a new conquest.

The Knight of Wands can also indicate a time when you need to follow your passions . . . or an adventure. If you've ever taken off on a whim or jumped into a new relationship without hesitation, you've experienced the vibe of this card. This marks a period when things are exciting! Ready, set, and go, go, GO!

Do keep in mind that there is also a potential for rash and reckless decisions. While there is nothing wrong with thrill-seeking, it doesn't hurt to think before you leap into a situation.

When symbolizing a person, the Knight of Wands is that sexy charmer who has a bit of an edge. The rock star or courageous leader who gets everyone amped up.

Other ways of looking at this card: adventures, a rogue, daredevil, travel, or cockiness.

When the card is reversed, this Knight can indicate impulse gone wrong. That moment when you know you shouldn't do it, but you do anyway. Regrets are sure to follow. A bit of restraint is needed. In relationships, this could be the person who goes from one romance to another with little regard for other people involved. That jerk who is only out to get what they want. Selfish desires. Or it can be the dud—that person who is full of charisma and turns out to lack passion.

It's also possible that the flame goes out before anything can really get started. Instead of moving forward with enthusiasm, you're pulling back, fearful of what may lie ahead. A lack of risks leads to stagnancy. A situation that goes nowhere fast.

How to embody the energy of this card: Play a game of Truth or Dare with a friend. Be ready to say yes to as many dares as you can. How does it feel to do something exciting and daring?

A question to ponder: *What is the one thing you wish you had taken a chance on in the past?*

Tarotcise

 Take the Knight of Wands out of the deck. Shuffle the cards and pull one randomly. Put that card in front of the Knight of Wands so the figure faces the other card. What does this card tell you about where the Knight of Wands is going? For example, if he's looking at the Four of Wands, he may be heading to a party. Looking at the Moon? Off to the desert! Try various cards and see what adventures lie ahead.

QUEEN of WANDS.

The Queen of Wands

Element: Fire

The Queen of Wands sits proudly on her throne, aware of her power, and ready to lead. She is the protectress of the realm, the brave feminine leader who inspires everyone around her. She's devoted to her creativity and always follows her passions. She has a fiery, intense nature that can sometimes be hot-tempered.

This card can indicate a person with a burning passion who encourages others. It can also be the mother lion who will do anything to keep others safe. But the Queen of Wands can also symbolize a time when you are tapped into your creativity. The muse is singing and what you're making now is truly exciting. A spark of inspiration grows into something beautiful.

Other ways of looking at this card: warmth, vitality, creative energy, personal power, and protection.

A selfish agenda lies underneath the heart of the Queen of Wands reversed. Instead of making sure everyone else is cared for, she wants to know, "What's in it for me?" This can also be a tough cookie, a total bitch, a person who wants to throw their weight around. Arrogance and cattiness create a bully who uses power to demean others. Sexuality unchecked, a loose person, or someone who is unavailable.

How to embody the energy of this card: What creative things did you enjoy doing as a child? Go back to a medium that you loved. Start nurturing that creative force again. Let it grow. See what it feels like to tend to your creative fire.

A question to ponder: *What does it mean to be creative?*

Tarotcise

Which world leaders embody the feminine leadership style of the Queen of Wands? List the ones who come to mind and situations where they best displayed that fiery, encouraging vibe.

KING of WANDS

The King of Wands

Element: Fire

The King of Wands perches on the edge of his throne. Is he ready to take a courageous stand? Or getting ready to kick back after achieving a major goal? This is the card of creative mastery, bold leadership, the inspirational thought leader who motivates people to be their very best. He's never afraid to take a risk or encourage others to do the same.

This card can indicate a time when you need to be fearless. You may be called to lead others by your courageous example. Or you may need to express yourself. Do not play small. Let your big heart lead the way and be willing to take a chance. The King of Wands can symbolize creative mastery or a flamboyant, confident person who stands out like a peacock.

Other ways of looking at this card: charisma, originality, drama, dominance, and masculine power.

When this card is reversed, the energy becomes timid, afraid to take a stand. Or it goes the other way: foolish, reckless, and arrogant. Pride gets in the way, and a fall follows. This can also be the unwise use of power or abuse of it. A dictator or someone who bends the rules to serve their ego. A lack of skill or unwillingness to accept responsibility at work. That time when you followed your passion blindly only to discover that doing so wasn't worthwhile. An old flame who refuses to move on. Leading with the wrong head.

How to embody the energy of this card: Look for a way you can motivate someone today. Give your child a pep talk. Cheer on your best friend. Stand up to a bully. Share an inspirational quote online.

A question to ponder: *What or who inspires you at this moment?*

Tarotcise

Choose a sport—any sport that you enjoy (if you don't like games, perhaps a dance competition). Now watch the coaches. Are they the King of Wands, or are they the King of Wands reversed? How are they motivating (or not) their team?

The Ace of Cups

ACE ♣ CUPS.

Element: Water

On the Ace of Cups, a beautiful vessel overflows with water. A dove dives headfirst into the cup with a holy communion wafer in its beak. This Ace hints at a new emotional beginning. It could be the start of a new relationship or a time when you are healing old wounds and beginning anew. The heart is open, ready to receive . . . and give equally. Love overflows. A divine connection begins. This is the moment of conception, birth, a proposal, marriage, or spiritual awakening.

When this card arrives, emotions are cleansed and purified. An opportunity for love is present, and you can proceed with an open heart and mind.

Other ways of looking at this card: intuition, new depths, intimacy, forgiveness, a gift, compassion, generosity, and self-expression.

When you reverse the Ace of Cups, nothing flows. The emotions become blocked, stunted, and closed off. This is classic emotional unavailability. It could signal a time when you are not ready to begin a relationship. Perhaps a bad experience has soured you, leaving you with trust issues. Or you may not be interested due to a lack of chemistry. You're "not feeling it," so you take a pass. The Ace of Cups reversed can also symbolize a relapse or time when old emotional issues come bubbling back to the surface. This reversal can indicate turning down an offer too.

How to embody the energy of this card: Let someone know that you care about them. Reach out and send your love. This could be through a letter, email, phone call, or text. What's important is that you send this love out without any thought of return.

A question to ponder: *How would your life feel if you approached everything with a completely open heart?*

Tarotcise

 Pull the Ace of Cups and the Five of Cups out of the deck. These are the only two Cups cards that show liquid. What does the pouring of the fluid mean in each card? Why do you think none of the other Cups cards show any water? Which Majors can you find that show the pouring of liquids? How might that be interpreted differently?

The Two of Cups

Element: Water

Two people come together in a toast, a sign of a connection being made. This is the card of attraction, that moment when you meet someone and are drawn in. Love at first sight. A meeting of the hearts and minds. This card indicates a developing relationship or two people forming a deeper bond.

Keep in mind that it does not always mean romance. Sometimes it's just two old friends getting together or a business meeting. Or a time when you can meet someone halfway—or make a compromise. Cooperation and teamwork bring results.

Other ways of looking at this card: truce, diplomacy, healing a relationship, marriage, handfasting, signing a contract, or a joint venture.

If you reverse the Two of Cups, you may see a disconnect or breakup. A relationship dissolves, and both people go their separate ways. Quarrels and betrayal. An inability to make a commitment. It's also possible that this reading could indicate a time when the relationship hits a rough spot—but gets through it. Much will depend on the other cards present.

How to embody the energy of this card: Today, get out and make eye contact with every person you encounter. Say hello to your barista, flirt with that interesting person, greet the mail carrier, listen to a loved one without checking your cell phone. Be completely present with everyone you meet.

A question to ponder: *How well do you connect with other people?*

Tarotcise

Look through the other Cups cards and find the ones where a figure is offering a Cup. Example: Six of Cups. What is being offered? Who is making the offer? How is the other person in the card responding? Journal your answers.

The Three of Cups

Element: Water

Celebration time! Harvest is here! Abundance and creativity are all around you. The Three of Cups indicates friendship and parties. A happy time well spent with people you like. A gathering of like-minded people. The support system that rallies around you just when you need it most. Festivities, fun, marriage, or birth. This card could also indicate a happy reunion with old pals or loved ones. Fertile ground or fertility rites.

Other ways of looking at this card: community, working together, dancing, circles of women, partying, high spirits, love triangle, polyamory, or threesome.

If you reverse the card, it's a sign that the party is over. Perhaps you receive bad news. Or maybe something you were counting on doesn't come to fruition. The Three of Cups reversed can also suggest overindulgence or binge drinking. Falling off the wagon. For relationship readings, this reversal can indicate unexpected pregnancy, interference from other people, a love triangle that has gone bad, infidelity, or a partner who wants to have their cake and eat it too. In some cases, this card could also signify frenemies or fair-weather friends, the kind who come around only when times are good. Betrayal among peers is another possibility.

How to embody the energy of this card: Gather your friends and paint the town red! A night spent with your most hilarious pals, laughing, and dancing is total Three of Cups energy!

A question to ponder: *When is the last time you had fun?*

Tarotcise

Find all the cards that indicate celebration in the tarot deck. How many are from the Cups suit? What other suits might show a festive scene? How are they similar? How are they different? Journal your findings.

The Four of Cups

Element: Water

On the Four of Cups, a hand with a cup makes an offer out of the blue. But the figure sits against the tree, not even glancing up. Do they even notice the cup? Are they disinterested? Or meditating? The Four of Cups indicates boredom, apathy, or disinterest. Even if the opportunities are excellent, you're not inspired to lift a finger. Maybe you want something other than what is being offered. Or perhaps you're an ingrate. This card can also indicate a time when the options are not thrilling. Of course, this can also represent a time of rest. Take time out. Sit on things for a minute before making a decision. In relationship questions, this card could also suggest emotional unavailability or celibacy.

Other ways of looking at this card: lethargy, laziness, no motivation, introspection, or cutting people off.

The reversed Four of Cups says: It's time for action! Say yes to new experiences and options. Get up and get moving. There is a lot to do, and everything is exciting again. Now you see the golden opportunity before you and are ready to do something about it. A new romantic interest or getting back into the dating game after a period away. A surprise offer that comes out of the blue.

How to embody the energy of this card: Sit with your back against a tree. Close your eyes. Breathe in deeply. Sit for a while. Can you quiet your mind? Or do you find meditation annoying? If you find that this practice makes you antsy, reflect on why that is so. Journal your thoughts.

A question to ponder: *What makes something boring to you?*

Tarotcise

Look at all the cards that are associated with the number four (including the Emperor). What do they all have in common?

The Five of Cups

Element: Water

The Five of Cups is rarely a welcome card to see in a tarot reading. After all, the cloaked figure seems to be in mourning. The interpretation is usually grief or a partial loss. Sadness, sorrow, and regrets. Focusing on the spilled cups, the figure is not able to see what's still standing. But should they move on, or should they allow more time for the grief to process? That will depend on the context of the question and the other cards surrounding it.

In some cases, the Five of Cups can advise that it is time to stop wallowing and begin rebuilding your life. But it can also say, "Hey, you're sad right now. Sit with this. Face those feelings." Grief is a hard taskmaster, but it is a part of life. When this card arrives, you must acknowledge the loss and how you feel before you start over.

Other ways of looking at this card: depression, hangover, emotional problems, feeling left out, abandonment, loss, pain, an inability to put the water under the bridge, or substance abuse.

If this card is reversed, the time is right to move on. A new opportunity presents itself. Don't let the past define your future. Instead, pick up what's left and start your new life. In some cases, this reversal can also indicate a refusal to face your problems. Instead of dealing with your loss, you're in denial. It also means an inability to get on with things because you assume the situation will get better on its own without your work. Recovery after relapse. Acceptance of disappointment.

How to embody the energy of this card: Think of a time in your life when you've suffered a loss. This could be the breakup of a relationship, the death of a loved one, or even the ending of a job. If you've never experienced grief, spend time with someone who has. Pay attention to your feelings. Can you sit with it, or do you turn away?

A question to ponder: *What have you learned from the sad times in your life?*

Tarotcise

 Both the Four of Cups and the Five of Cups have three cups in front of them. Neither character seems to notice the other cups around them. What might this have to say about the figures? What can be learned by examining the three cups . . . and the ones they are not acknowledging?

Journal your thoughts.

The Six of Cups

Element: Water

The lovely Six of Cups is a reminder of all the good things from the past, as well as the sweet moments right here in the present. The Six of Cups indicates a time when you can enjoy the simple pleasures. Stop and smell the roses. Security and joy. The happiness that comes from memories or from a loved one from the past.

This card can also indicate old-fashioned courtship. A romantic partner that comes bearing gifts and flowers. An opportunity to get to know a new person. The melding of two hearts. It's also sometimes seen as a card that represents children and home, bringing joy . . . or time of innocence.

Other ways of looking at this card: nostalgia, bliss, charity, hometown, pregnancy, virtue, goodwill, community, and family matters.

Ever get so hung up on the past that you cannot see the great things that are happening right now? That's what this reversal means. Clinging to the old and familiar. Stuck in the comfort zone. Or it can also indicate a reality check—something happens that brings you right here, right now. In some cases, the reversed Six of Cups can show the old family of origin drama still producing problems today, or a past love that can't get the hint.

How to embody the energy of this card: Spend time with elders asking about the good old days. What was life like when they were young? What experiences impacted who they are today? Also, go through old photo albums and reminisce about what was happening at that time. Another great way to embody this card: call up an old friend.

A question to ponder: *What lessons from the past are you carrying forward?*

Tarotcise

Find all the cards with houses in them. Houses can symbolize security and achievement. How do the houses play out in each card? What about the building in the Tower? What might that have to say about security? Write down your thoughts.

The Seven of Cups

Element: Water

On the Seven of Cups, a shadowy figure stands in front of a group of goblets, some laden with gold. Why are they hesitating? What are they waiting for? This card symbolizes decisions, choices, and the uncertainty about which one to make. Are the options for real, or are they fantasy? It may be hard to tell.

This card marks a time when you must choose wisely. That begins by examining each opportunity with great care. Look beneath the surface. What is really being offered? All that glitters may not be gold.

The Seven of Cups can also indicate daydreaming, wishful thinking, and getting your head stuck in the clouds. While there is nothing wrong with fantasizing, you must watch out that you don't lose track of reality.

Other ways of looking at this card: delusions, distractions, laziness, disorganized, clutter, excess, impracticality, creative thinking, and unrealistic people.

Reverse the Seven of Cups, and suddenly you can see clearly. Or a decision is made for you. It can also indicate a time when you are so unsure of yourself that you become paralyzed, hoping someone else will take responsibility for making choices. Illusions are removed. A time of action, not dreaming. Taking your dreams and turning them into a reality.

How to embody the energy of this card: Put yourself in a situation where you know making a decision will be challenging. For me, that's in a bookstore! I could get lost for hours trying to decide which one to pick.

A question to ponder: *What might be the consequences of the choice you are about to make?*

Tarotcise

What's in the cups? Explore each cup. Reflect on what each one holds and what those symbols could mean. Journal your answers.

The Eight of Cups

Element: Water

The Eight of Cups signals moving on. Whatever you've accomplished, you must leave that behind and venture off in a new direction. This could be a time in your life when you feel that you need something different. Or perhaps you're taking a time-out to search your soul. Don't look back. Look ahead and trust that whatever you are about to do will bring growth.

The seeker of knowledge. A period of reflection. Travel. All of these are possibilities too. In my own tarot practice, I've also seen this card as a warning to walk away, no matter how good the situation may appear. That has happened in certain friendships: I asked about the person and pulled this card. Both times, I ignored the advice and learned a brutal lesson. So when I see this card arrive, I know that moving on is sometimes a preventative measure.

Other ways of looking at this card: letting go, moving to a new home, downsizing, choosing a minimalist life, restlessness, endings, and change.

Let's reverse this card: Go back. You're not done. A situation is unfinished, and you must take care of the details before you can leave. This card can indicate returning to the past, either to seek closure or because you feel that you are not able to move on. Going back to that old relationship that isn't healthy? Yep. That. It can also indicate a situation where you feel stuck due to circumstances. Example: you're trying to leave town, but a massive storm cancels all flights. Not much you can do except wait things out until you get the all-clear.

How to embody the energy of this card: Think about something in your life that is indeed done, but yet you hold on to it. For example, a grudge from twenty years ago. An old friend who feels draining. A project that is complete but you're fussing over the details. Move on. Let it go. Start looking ahead to a new beginning.

A question to ponder: *What alerts you when it's time to go?*

Tarotcise

Look at the way the Cups are stacked. There is a group of five and a group of three. Why are they stacked this way? Why not put them into one neat pyramid? What does this tell you about the card?

The Nine of Cups

Element: Water

The Nine of Cups is often referred to as the "wish card," which means folks love to see this one pop up in a tarot reading! After all, who doesn't want to get their wishes fulfilled? This card can indeed indicate realizing your heart's desire, but also that feeling when everything seems to be lining up beautifully. The proverbial ducks in a row. Your universe is now set up for good things to happen, but know that this is not magic—it's because you focused and did your part. You put yourself in the best position possible.

This card can also indicate celebrations and happiness. A time when life is good and joy is in abundant supply. Everything that you need is present. Friends and well-wishers surround and support you. Life is improving. All is well. Enjoy your good fortune!

Other ways of looking at this card: satisfaction, indulgence, parties, smugness, sensual delights, and bragging rights.

If a reversal turns up, be careful what you wish for—you may get it. Sometimes the things we want aren't necessarily good for us. Therefore, the reversed Nine of Cups suggests that you examine your motivation. Why do you want what you want? What do you hope to gain? Is this goal healthy or something that may cause you harm? This reversal can also indicate too much of the good life. Overdoing the partying leads to sloth and ruin.

How to embody the energy of this card: Hold the card in your hand and close your eyes. Think back to a time when a wish came true. How did you feel? What steps did you take to make this happen? Or did it seem to show up out of the blue? Consider the role that magic and intention play in your life, and journal your thoughts.

A question to ponder: *What do you really want right now, at this time?*

Tarotcise

 Nine is a number of endings and completion. How does that fit in with the happy Nine of Cups?

The Ten of Cups

Element: Water

The Ten of Cups is the happy ending card! Peace, joy, and prosperity. Happiness is here, and you're deeply supported. This card can indicate the joyful conclusion to a goal or any reason to celebrate (wedding, birth, graduation, birthday, etc.). It symbolizes domestic bliss and family harmony too. Relationships are moving in a positive direction. The family you always wanted is possible. You're surrounded by people who love you. You're secure. You have that feeling of "having it all."

Other ways of looking at this card: family reunion, peace, a peace treaty, building or buying a home, children, abundance, expanding your family, welcoming neighbors, or a safe neighborhood.

All of that good energy falls apart when the Ten of Cups is reversed. This reading indicates family drama. Quarrels with loved ones. Divorce. A feud with your kin. Or an inability to move out of the family home. Good fortune is still here, but perhaps you are unable to see it or enjoy it. In that case, the joy becomes muted.

How to embody the energy of this card: Spend time with family members you love. This can be your birth family or chosen family. Soak up those good vibes!

A question to ponder: *What does family mean to you?*

Tarotcise

Compare this card to the Ten of Pentacles, which also contains a family. How are these cards similar . . . and different? Which family do you prefer and why? Write down your thoughts.

The Page of Cups

Element: Water

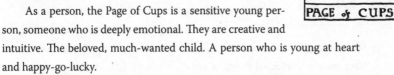

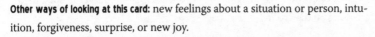

Pages can indicate messages, and in the case of the Page of Cups, the news is favorable. This could be an announcement you've been waiting on or a love note. It can also symbolize the beginning of a romantic situation. A crush or infatuation. That first flutter of the heart, and suddenly you're falling in love!

As a person, the Page of Cups is a sensitive young person, someone who is deeply emotional. They are creative and intuitive. The beloved, much-wanted child. A person who is young at heart and happy-go-lucky.

Other ways of looking at this card: new feelings about a situation or person, intuition, forgiveness, surprise, or new joy.

If you reverse this card, you get a spoiled brat. A manipulator who uses emotions to get their way. Or a person who lives in a fantasy world, unable to cope with reality. The Page of Cups reversed can also indicate news that makes you sad. Or a relationship that never quite gets off the ground. In some cases, it can mean an infatuation or obsession that is not returned.

How to embody the energy of this card: Send a love note to someone. This could be a family member, your current partner, or a secret crush.

A question to ponder: *What risks have you taken for love?*

Tarotcise

The Page of Cups is one of the thirteen "stage" cards in the tarot deck—cards that show figures standing on what appears to be a stage. The horizontal line represents a painted backdrop. Find the other stage cards in the deck. What play might they be rehearsing?

KNIGHT of CUPS.

The Knight of Cups

Element: Water

The Knight of Cups is the romantic hero, the person guided by their heart. Romantic adventures are on the way when this card shows up in a reading. This can symbolize a time when you are ready to let your heart lead the way. Perhaps you want to pursue a relationship. Or maybe you're taking a chance on doing something you love. Feelings and emotions are active at this time. Express your heart!

This card can also represent a person who is romantic in nature, gushy, and sensitive. They respond deeply to life and beauty and can get easily affected by other people's moods. In some cases, this could be someone with a big imagination who lacks the practicality needed to get anything off the ground.

Other ways of looking at this card: compassion, imagination, visionary, the Knight in Shining Armor, Prince Charming, a poet or artist, or dreamer.

The overemotional, unrealistic person who can't seem to get a grip on reality is classic Knight of Cups reversed. They don't follow through on promises. Instead, they are stuck in a fantasy world. When things get too real, they sulk. The Knight of Cups reversed can also indicate a time when you have trouble listening to your heart. You may choose to tune it out, much to your regret later. An inability to take action on your instincts.

How to embody the energy of this card: When have you acted on your feelings? Perhaps you made a move on that person you fancied. Or you said yes to that job on a whim . . . and loved it so much you stayed. I purchased my first tarot deck impulsively, and I've been in love ever since. That's Knight of Cups energy!

A question to ponder: *What is your heart telling you right now?*

Tarotcise

What are some of the classic romantic heroes or heroines in literature that may fit the Knight of Cups profile?

QUEEN of CUPS.

The Queen of Cups

Element: Water

The loving, tenderhearted Queen of Cups is entirely in tune with how she feels. Not just emotionally but also intuitively. She trusts her gut and never ignores how situations or people make her feel. She is psychic and empathic, which means she can easily read into other people's moods. Her sweet nature means she tends to be kind toward others. Compassion and gentleness are her natural state of being.

This card can symbolize a time when you must tune in to your feelings. Are you aware of how situations are affecting you? Or you may be ready to open up to someone—perhaps a romantic partner. It can also indicate nurturing others. Maybe you're taking care of a loved one or involved in work where you nurture others, such as a teacher or nurse. Emotions are strong at this time.

Other ways of looking at this card: psychic, emotional depth, sixth sense, caretaker, advisor, or spiritual maturity.

If you reverse the Queen of Cups, she becomes ungrounded, moody, and a drama queen. Instead of trusting her feelings, she's full of doubt. This reversal can signal a time when your emotions get the best of you . . . or you ignore your instincts.

How to embody the energy of this card: The next time you're in any place around other people, sit quietly and notice what you feel. What vibe do you pick up? Now, go into another situation that may be upsetting, say a sad movie. Let your feelings out completely. Allow for a good cry if you need to. Journal your thoughts.

A question to ponder: *How do your feelings affect your decision-making?*

Tarotcise

The Queen of Cups and Queen of Wands are both genuinely in touch with their desires, but how might that show up differently?

KING of CUPS.

The King of Cups

Element: Water

Ah, the King of Love! The wise, caring King of Cups always looks out for everyone. He's sincere and loving, a dependable caretaker who always has a kind word for all. Known for his benevolence, people flock to him. He's an advice-giver, a provider, and a lover. This card can represent a person who makes everyone feel safe and loved. The King of Cups is the mature lover who can always be counted on for romance or to handle situations with calmness.

This card can indicate a situation where emotional growth is possible. A time when you're healing the old wounds and discovering new layers of love. Instead of force, love rules all.

Other ways of looking at this card: tolerance, mastery of the emotions, experience, healer, therapist, the kindly parent, navigating rough seas, travel, diplomacy, and plenty of fish in the sea.

The reversed King of Cups is immature and shallow. This can be a person who cannot be trusted, especially when the going gets tough. Instead of keeping the peace, they stir the pot. Or it can be someone emotionally unavailable or needy. In some cases, this reversal can symbolize a situation where control is lost, and everything becomes unstable. Addiction and over-indulgence. A person who is "lost at sea," unable to find their moral compass.

How to embody the energy of this card: Think of the show *Father Knows Best*. In that show, the father figure gently guided his children. Look for other sources of mature, caring individuals in popular culture or in your life. Mr. Rogers is my favorite King of Cups!

A question to ponder: *How do you navigate difficult emotional times for yourself or others?*

Tarotcise

 Both the Page of Cups and King of Cups have fish in their cards. What might that symbolize? Journal your thoughts about the fish in these cards and why the other two Cups Courts don't have live fish in their cards. (Psst . . . look for the hidden fishes in the Knight and Queen.)

The Ace of Swords

Element: Air

The Ace of Swords is the big break or breakthrough. That aha moment when the clouds part and you can move forth with confidence. This card indicates clarity, a fresh start, an exciting idea, the pursuit of truth. This could be a mentally stimulating offer or a challenge that leads to a more significant opportunity. It can also signal a time when you must be ethical, no matter what. In some cases, it can also warn of the beginning of a conflict.

When this card shows up in a reading, be ready to think, act, and, in some cases, fight. Carpe diem!

Other ways of looking at this card: taking control, mental force, overcoming obstacles, seizing power, passing a test, righting a wrong, and objectivity.

Reversed, this Ace is an idea that goes nowhere fast. Momentum is lost. Nothing can get off the ground. This reversal could also indicate the end of a conflict or a surrender. In some cases, it's an inability to fight for what's right. Cowardice. The reversed Ace of Swords can also indicate harsh words that cut to the bone. A lie for no good reason. The breakdown before the breakthrough.

How to embody the energy of this card: The next time you get a big idea, act on it immediately! Song lyrics in your head? Write 'em down! Got a flash of inspiration about a cool invention? Research and see if it's been done!

A question to ponder: *What is your truth?*

Tarotcise

What do you think it means when all of the Aces come up in a tarot reading?

The Two of Swords

Element: Air

The Two of Swords signals indecision. Take time out, away from it all. The quiet will do you good. Sometimes we need to isolate ourselves to get perspective. This card can also indicate a deadlock—a situation that is not moving. An opposition or stalemate. No one budges. Depending on the other cards, it can also mean a truce . . . or a time when you refuse to take sides.

Another interpretation is blocked emotions. A barrier. Emotional unavailability. The heart chakra is closed down, and nothing can get in.

In some cases, this card can also indicate weighing options. Meditating on the possibilities.

Other ways of looking at this card: avoiding an issue, denying your feelings, tuning out, inability to see the truth, fear, denial.

The reversed Two of Swords says the balance is lost. Reality sets in. The blindfold slips. Now you can see what's happening and what to do. You can no longer deny what's going on. The problem cannot be avoided. A decision is made for you. Or the time-out is over and now you must get back into the game.

How to embody the energy of this card: The next time you're facing a decision, sit quietly and meditate on your options. What does your inner wisdom have to say?

A question to ponder: *In what way do you avoid unpleasantness in your life?*

Tarotcise

Both the Two of Swords and Eight of Cups feature Moons, symbols of reflection. Both figures are also taking time out. In what way is this similar? In what way are the two cards different? How are they stepping away? Write down your ideas.

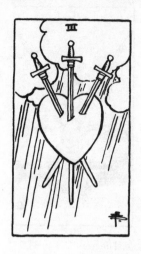

The Three of Swords

Element: Air

No one likes to see the Three of Swords. It symbolizes heartbreak, pain, sorrow, and loss. Emotions are raw. Much healing is needed. This is a betrayal that cuts deep, a time when you've been hurt beyond measure.

In relationships, this card can indicate separation or divorce. A relationship comes to an ugly conclusion. Your emotional world has been turned upside down and inside out. Something or someone in your life is causing you great sadness.

This card can also indicate that you're thinking of letting someone down. Before you ghost that person, think about how your actions might impact them.

Other ways of looking at this card: loneliness, distance, abandonment, a stormy time, infidelity, rejection, and war.

The reversed Three of Swords signals the wounds are beginning to heal. The storm is over, and the air is clear. You can assess the damage done and move on. In some cases, this reversal can also indicate avoiding pain. You won't let go of a situation because you're afraid that it will hurt.

How to embody the energy of this card: Call to mind a time when you've been brokenhearted. This could be from losing a relationship or getting fired from a job you loved. Sit with the feeling. Do not push it away. Breathe deeply and send yourself as much love as possible.

A question to ponder: *When has your heart been broken wide open?*

Tarotcise

Soap operas are a great place to find tarot; there is always drama! Tune in to a soap opera and count up all the times the themes of betrayal and heartbreak show up. Journal your findings.

The Four of Swords

Element: Air

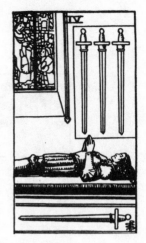

Rest up! That's what the Four of Swords seems to say. This card shows a figure chilling out on top of a casket in a church setting. No, it doesn't mean death. Instead, it's a sign that you must recuperate after a battle. Heal. Take time away from the daily grind. This will restore your balance. If life has been hard, resting up will do your soul right.

Another way to look at this card is contemplation. If you're pondering a decision, meditating on it longer may be the best approach. Do not rush to judgement. Instead, quiet the mind and give yourself permission to explore the possibilities.

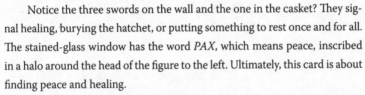

Notice the three swords on the wall and the one in the casket? They signal healing, burying the hatchet, or putting something to rest once and for all. The stained-glass window has the word *PAX*, which means peace, inscribed in a halo around the head of the figure to the left. Ultimately, this card is about finding peace and healing.

In some cases, this card can indicate hospitalization or a period of convalescing. I've also seen this card as "Sleeping Beauty," or waiting around for someone else to wake you up.

Other ways of looking at this card: planning, preparation, retreat, ashram, stillness.

Reversed, this card says: You're back in action! The time for rest has ended. Life gets busy again. You're ready to make a move. Get back in the game. Recovery is complete. Come out of a period of isolation and back into the world. In some cases, this reversal can indicate feeling antsy or unable to relax.

How to embody the energy of this card: Pick a day when you do nothing at all. Sit around. Read a book. Nap. Ahhh...

A question to ponder: *Are you getting enough rest?*

Tarotcise

Find all the cards with stained-glass windows. What hidden messages might you discover in those cards, if any? Stained glass can also indicate perception. What might the figures in these cards be seeing, and how might their opinion be clear or not?

The Five of Swords

Element: Air

I have to admit that the Five of Swords is my least favorite card in the deck. The turbulent skies, people crying, and the smirking figure do not give me a warm fuzzy. This is the card of cruelty, deception, and conquest. Everything about the Five of Swords screams malice! While an element of victory is present, it's a hollow one that is achieved only through dishonest means.

I've seen this card come up for hostile takeovers of businesses, political sabotage, and online scams. It's always a sign of trouble. If it shows up in a reading, know that someone is up to no good and they don't give a fig about whom they hurt.

Other ways of looking at this card: dishonor, hostility, criminal activity, rip-off, abuse, and a lack of morals.

When the Five of Swords turns up reversed, all lies come out into the open. A saboteur is exposed. Conflicts end, and peace returns. Someone is caught in the act; their nefarious plans fall apart. A chance to make something right again. A truce. Or the defeat of a treacherous and powerful foe.

How to embody the energy of this card: Think of a time when someone pulled the wool over your eyes or used unfair means to win. How did you feel when that happened? Now, how might you feel if you were the one using dishonesty as a means to achieve your goals?

A question to ponder: *What does it mean when people say that all is fair in love and war? Is that true?*

Tarotcise

Grab all of the Fives out of your tarot deck. Even the Majors, including the cards that can be broken down into a Five (for example, which Major is 14?). Five is considered a severe number. What are the challenges in each Five? How have you worked through these challenges in your own life?

The Six of Swords

Element: Air

On the Six of Swords, the three people in the boat are sailing on. The energy between them seems forlorn. This card symbolizes moving on after a loss. Support is present. The Six of Swords indicates a time of transition. It may feel difficult. Perhaps you don't want to leave the old situation. Or you're hurting and need time to mourn. Maybe you feel uncertain about what's up ahead. Whatever the case may be, you must trust the journey before you. You've learned so much from past events. The changes ahead will be for your highest good.

For now, do not look back. Dry your tears, gather your loved ones, and begin the trek to a new place. This card can also indicate physical travel, especially around water. In some cases, it can mean exile, a time when you're being forced to leave a situation.

Other ways of looking at this card: refugees, sadness, picking up the pieces of your life, travel, a physical move, change of scenery, smooth sailing ahead, we're all in the same boat.

The Six of Swords reversed says: you're stuck. You cannot seem to gain any traction. Cycles are being repeated. You keep going back to the same thing again and again, even though you know it's not healthy. The support you need isn't there, or maybe you're not asking for it. If you're unhappy with your present company, this may be a sign that you need to "get out of the boat." Travel woes. The inability to find a peaceful solution to current problems.

How to embody the energy of this card: Is there something in your world that you need to leave behind? An old thought? A toxic relationship? Doing it may feel hard, but with support, you can. This is the Six of Swords energy: seeking help so you can move on.

A question to ponder: *What might your life look like if you chose a new direction?*

Tarotcise

 The travel cards in tarot are the Six of Swords, Eight of Cups, and Eight of Wands. All classics. Are there any other cards that you might associate with a trip? Which ones? Why? Journal your answers.

The Seven of Swords

Element: Air

Ah, tricky Seven of Swords! Look at the dude gingerly stepping away from a tent, a sneer on his face as he makes off with a bundle of swords. On the one hand, this card indicates a time for cunning. On the other, it can symbolize a theft. What it means will be determined by the question. This card can show stealth, a time when you can pull off a great feat right under the noses of others. Folks are amazed that you were able to do it! But it can also indicate sneakiness—as in sneaking around with a new partner and getting away with it. In some cases, it might suggest that you're making some progress but may not be able to get it all done neatly.

Again, the theft side of this card is another interpretation. A thief walks off with your goods. A no-good hussy steals your partner. A sly salesman rips you off. They get away with it . . . and feel no remorse. In that case, the card serves as a warning to watch your back.

A true story: a client kept getting this card in the "environment" position of her reading. "But I live in a good neighborhood," she said. I told her that a robbery can happen in any place. The next time I saw her, she told me that she did indeed get robbed, right outside *my* house. You can't make this stuff up!

Other ways of looking at this card: independence, avoiding drama, walking on eggshells, slipping under the radar, treason, and running away from your responsibilities.

The stolen objects are returned when this card turns up reversed. A thief is caught. The jig is up, the scam revealed. Or you see right through a situation, know it's bogus, and get the heck out before you can get burned. In some cases, this reversal indicates returning to the scene of the crime. A confession. Someone reveals the truth about themselves. In other words, the reversal shows the facts, the prevention of a crime, or the act of getting caught.

How to embody the energy of this card: What is the most impossible thing you could do right now? Do it.

A question to ponder: *Is it ever okay to bend the truth?*

Tarotcise

 Take the Seven of Cups, Seven of Pentacles, Seven of Wands, and Seven of Swords out of the deck. You'll notice that all of the figures seem to be hesitating. It's hard to see what's really happening when you think about it. Why is the Seven of Cups standing in front of those Cups? What is the figure in the Seven of Pentacles doing? Are they resting or admiring their handiwork? Is the character in the Seven of Wands pushing back or starting a conflict? Do you think the guy in the Seven of Swords is moving on or looking back and thinking of stopping? Ponder the possibilities here.

The Eight of Swords

Element: Air

On the Eight of Swords, a woman is blindfolded and loosely bound, alone except for the swords around her. How did she get here? No one knows. That answer comes from within. When this card arrives, it can indicate a time when you feel stuck, lost, or isolated. But if you really think about it, you see that your binds are loose. You can get out. Your leaving begins by examining how you got into this position in the first place. Once you do that, you'll see the way out.

The Eight of Swords symbolizes that feeling of being trapped by your circumstances. This impression doesn't last forever, but it sure feels like it. Once you do the work, you'll shake off the feeling and move on. But until you do that, you remain stuck. You—and only you—can free yourself.

Sometimes, depending on the question, this card can indicate a time when you get bound up by someone else. That jealous partner who won't let you out of the house, that job that sucks but you need the bread, or that boss who lays down oppressive rules. In those cases, the card says you're being forced to remain in a situation and need to start looking for an exit, even if leaving feels scary.

This card can also represent an initiation. Many initiation rites require being blindfolded and bound; cutting the ties and removing the blindfold symbolize a rebirth. It's like being in the cocoon before you spread your wings.

Other ways of looking at this card: limitation, tightening the belt, isolation, being controlled, the damsel in distress, victim, lack of freedom, losing your power, or being "tied up" with too many responsibilities.

If this card is reversed, you're free! You found the way out. The blindfold slips off, the binds loosen, and you can leave your situation. Like Houdini, you are able to get out of a jam. This reversal can also indicate a time when you see things clearly. You know what to do. The limits are off. You can transcend your situation. The exit is straight ahead.

How to embody the energy of this card: No, I won't ask you to tie yourself up! Instead, put yourself into an uncomfortable position. Maybe go to a strip club. Or put on a pair of too-tight pants. Have fun with this! See what you think when you get yourself into something that doesn't feel good. Now get out of it.

A question to ponder: *In what ways do you limit yourself?*

Tarotcise

According to Rachel Pollack, the Eight of Swords is one of the "Gate" cards, certain cards that "act as a Gate to a special awareness." Grab a copy of *78 Degrees of Wisdom* and find the passage on Gate cards. What are the other Gate cards? How do they each function as a gate? In what way do they do it differently? Journal your thoughts.

The Nine of Swords

Element: Air

Worry. Anxiety. Nightmares. The Nine of Swords card conjures such words. The figure sitting in bed, head in hands, swords piercing the back—every one of those symbols indicates losing sleep over a situation. Maybe you've been betrayed or suffered a loss. Or perhaps you're dealing with a mental health crisis. Whatever the case may be, the suffering is real. The Universe is getting personal with you.

The Nine of Swords indicates the things that go bump in the night. Situations that feel like a nightmare, times when you feel so alone. When this card arrives, you must not suffer in silence—seek help. Get support so you can see the possible closure. Sometimes, this card can indicate hospitalization or rehab.

Other ways of looking at this card: mental stress, getting stabbed in the back, insomnia, dark night of the soul, or hospitals.

The reversed Nine of Swords suggests the nightmare comes to an end. Anxieties cease. Support arrives. Healing. Recuperation. You are seeing the light at the end of the tunnel. At last, there is hope.

How to embody the energy of this card: Focus on something that makes you feel anxious. For me, that's the news. Turn on any news program, and it won't take long before you're deep in Nine of Swords.

A question to ponder: *What keeps you up at night?*

Tarotcise

Both the Four of Swords and Nine of Swords can indicate hospitals. What type of treatment might the figure be receiving? If you combine these cards with different Court cards, what role might they play in the healing? For example, is the Queen of Swords a surgeon? Might the Knight of Cups be an addiction counselor?

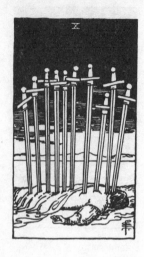

The Ten of Swords

Element: Air

The Ten of Swords depicts the total ending. A situation comes to a painful close, but fear not: a new beginning is ahead. There is a bright sunrise, a symbol of a fresh start. What's done is done. Accept the ending as best as you can and prepare to move on.

Take a peek at the figure's hand. I'm a yoga teacher, so that position of the hand is familiar to me; it's a mudra called the *jnana mudra*. Mudras are symbolic hand positions or ritual gestures. In Sanskrit, the word *mudra* means "seal." These hand positions are intended to help with the flow of energy in the physical and spiritual bodies. The jnana mudra is the wisdom mudra, so think about this for a minute: the bloodless knives show pain through the mental body, and the mudra shows the flow of energy through the physical and spiritual bodies as well as wisdom. This image shows you that this card is actually not that scary because it's actually an indicator of a cycle fully completed.

Sometimes this card can indicate a betrayal. Someone stabs you in the back. A massive disappointment. Loss. In a reading about health, this can mean back trouble.

Other ways of looking at this card: hitting rock bottom, melodrama, psychic attack, exhaustion, martyrdom, "woe is me," and the downward spiral before the rise.

When this card is reversed, it signals the worst is over. You made it! You can pick up and go about your business. The swords fall out of your back. Like a phoenix, you can *rise*. Healing. Forgiveness. In some cases, this reversal can indicate a refusal to accept an ending. Even though it's evident that something is over, you hang on.

How to embody the energy of this card: The next time you're dealing with a loss or something painful, look for the sunrise. That might be the lessons in the situation or the promise of a fresh start. Or as Mr. Rogers said: "Look for the helpers."

A question to ponder: *How do you deal with loss?*

Tarotcise

 I love tarot combinations. Putting two cards together can show a mini-story. What might be the mini-story of the Nine of Swords followed by the Ten of Swords? How about when you put the Ten of Swords before the Nine of Swords? Or turn them upside down? Play with this combo.

PAGE of SWORDS.

The Page of Swords

Element: Air

The Page of Swords can signify important news. A swift change may be on the way. Brace yourself. You must be alert for signs of trouble. Be prepared to defend yourself . . . or to solve a problem. This could also mean a time when truth clears the air. You can right a wrong at last.

As a person, this Page is the champion. A contender. A young person who is bright and mentally agile. Or a messenger who brings challenges.

This card can also mean a new mental beginning, the start of school, going back to school, a child who says what is on their mind.

Other ways of looking at this card: an analytic approach to issues, using your mind, cutting a cord, cutting edge, technology, and new ways of thinking.

Sometimes the reversed Page of Swords represents a young person who brings drama. A troublemaker. Someone who stirs the pot deliberately. A juvenile delinquent. But it can also mean a white lie or fib. Lack of ethics. Questionable morals. Or not learning the lesson. In some cases, this could be petty theft.

How to embody the energy of this card: Swords are the Air element, and they rule thoughts. The Page of Swords loves to learn and prefers a challenge. Study something that challenges you. For some, that might be physics. For others, computer repair. Stimulate your mind with something new!

A question to ponder: *How do you adapt to sudden changes?*

Tarotcise

Watch the news. How are the journalists reporting the news? Are they objective, especially when covering difficult subjects? Find a particular journalist who can deliver the critical stuff but remain neutral. How do they make you feel versus someone who seems to have a bias? That's Page of Swords energy.

KNIGHT of SWORDS .

The Knight of Swords

Element: Air

The Knight of Swords charges in, ready to do battle. Nothing stops him. This card can indicate a period when you must take the reins and move forth, even though the odds may seem high. This is the warrior in tarot. The hero. The sharpshooter. He's blunt, direct, and fearless. Logic is his weapon, and he uses the truth to cut through the crap. Whether this card symbolizes you or a person who is affecting the situation, one thing is for sure: words will not be minced.

That being said, this card can also indicate a lack of diplomacy. Or a bull in a china shop. That person who rushes in without knowing the situation and shoots off their mouth. It can also mean a time when you must act first, ask questions later.

Other ways of looking at this card: bluntness, dominance, rudeness, the brutal critic, sarcasm, a challenge, or trying to make a point.

If you reverse this Knight, suddenly he shows restraint. Instead of rushing in, he holds back. That could be due to wisely assessing the situation first . . . or cowardice. The reading depends on the context of the question and other cards involved. Sometimes this reversal can indicate a person who uses the truth to harm others or who lies habitually. It can also be the card of the criminal. Ill-tempered. Someone who has no sensitivity or logic. A buffoon. That person who puts up nasty remarks on social media and lives to regret it later.

How to embody the energy of this card: Engage in a lively debate. Speak your truth!

A question to ponder: *When is truth a weapon that fixes, and when can it cause harm?*

 Tarotcise

If the Page of Swords and Knight of Swords were in a battle, what roles would they play?

The Queen of Swords

Element: Air

The earnest Queen of Swords can create clarity in any given situation. She sees through the clouds right down to the facts. She's astute, clever, and intellectual. You can count on her to deliver a well-timed witty retort that will quickly shut down any nonsense. It's not easy to fool her. If this card shows up in your reading, it can indicate a time when you're sharp as a tack or need to be. You must size up a situation and be ready to take a logical approach.

Situations need you to be straightforward. No holding back. If this card symbolizes a person, they hold the qualities mentioned above: a no-nonsense, truthful individual who gets to the bottom of things quickly. This card can also represent a widow or someone who has suffered a significant loss.

Other ways of looking at this card: nurturing your ideas, judgement, cleverness, living by your wits, shrewdness, a lack of pretense, what you see is what you get.

This can be a tough reversal to see. Often the Queen of Swords reversed is interpreted as a deceiver or bitch. A person who won't deal with their feelings. Someone who doesn't acknowledge grieving. A cold, heartless individual. The Queen of Swords reversed brings drama and sorrow. They might have a hidden agenda. The Nurse Ratched or *Mommie Dearest* archetype.

How to embody the energy of this card: Take a direct approach to any situation you're dealing with today. Be candid, logical, and clearheaded. Let your experience help you make sound judgements.

A question to ponder: *Are you sincere when it counts?*

Tarotcise

Practice playing the role of each Queen in one day. For example, you might go into Queen of Wands mode as you make time to work on a creative project while later you're full-on Queen of Cups when you're spending time with the family. Try on Queen of Swords when you're dealing with that telemarketer and channel the Queen of Pentacles while you balance your checkbook. Have fun with this! Notice when you have to play each Queen in different areas of your life. How does it feel to move between the different energies of the Queens?

The King of Swords

Element: Air

The King of Swords is the thought leader, the wise counselor who offers impartial advice to any given situation. He is logical, intelligent, and ethical. He creates the laws or upholds them. This is the person who leads with their head. At times, they may challenge your beliefs. They are here to make you think . . . and behave. This King is the one you want to see in an emergency situation, for they always remain calm, no matter what is going on around them. Mr. Spock is the archetype for this logical fellow.

The King of Swords could be a person in your life who is a master of reason. Or this card may symbolize a time when you must be impartial. You may need to put your feelings aside and follow the highest ethical standards. Communicate well and be sure to remain fair in all of your dealings.

Other ways of looking at this card: analytical, clearing mental fog, mastering your thinking, lofty ideals, a wise judge or attorney, and ethics.

Reversed, this King loses his integrity and becomes an unsympathetic type who cannot be moved, no matter what. A bully. The criminal mastermind à la *The Godfather*—cruel, manipulative, and will use whatever means they can to achieve their goal. Coldness. A lack of empathy. An abuser.

How to embody the energy of this card: When making an important decision, see whether you can take all of your emotions out of the equation. Look for the most logical route. If necessary, research your options thoroughly.

A question to ponder: *Who inspires you through their shining example of integrity?*

Tarotcise

If the four members of the Swords Court were in a *Perry Mason* drama, who would be who?

The Ace of Pentacles

Element: Earth

On the Ace of Pentacles, a hand appears out of the sky, holding a giant gold coin above a garden. This Ace shows a path opening up before you, one that could change your financial future for the better. Ahead, everything is blossoming. Say yes to the opportunity and begin moving toward a brighter, abundant life.

This card signifies a new financial beginning. A change is offered—perhaps a new job or promotion. A fresh financial start. You can get on the right path once and for all. This card marks the potential for prosperity. Good news about money. It may also indicate a financial improvement that comes from an unexpected source.

Other ways of looking at this card: material success, growth, a promising opportunity, a seed, a gift, and being in the right place at the right time.

Reversed, the Ace of Pentacles becomes financial insecurity. You can't seem to get on the right foot, no matter what you do. The choices are slim. Unwise decisions create cracks in the foundation. This reversal can also mean squandering your money through poor investments or gambling. Or an opportunity that doesn't pan out. A job offer or promotion with little to gain. In some cases, it could indicate getting downsized or demoted.

How to embody the energy of this card: Anytime you make a change with your finances—a new job, side hustle, or budget—you're in Ace of Pentacles mode.

A question to ponder: *How can you improve your cash flow?*

Tarotcise

If you look at the Aces, the offers seem to come out of the clouds. Where are they coming from? What spirits, guides, or other energies might be bringing the offer? Journal your answers.

The Two of Pentacles

Element: Earth

On the Two of Pentacles, the figure juggles two massive coins. His unsteady feet and expression of uncertainty suggest instability. Instead of feeling secure, he's doing a juggling act. Decisions around money must be made with great care. The Two of Pentacles means stretching the dollar during hard times or borrowing from Peter to pay Paul. A time when you have to do whatever it takes to make ends meet.

The ships in the background show the potential for change or travel. How can you find steadiness when things seem to be moving in different directions? If you need to travel or move, how will you prepare?

This card can also indicate changing values. What was important to you at one time is now in flux. An ethical dilemma. If you're trying to make a decision, the card may advise weighing options carefully. You may be comparing apples to oranges.

Other ways of looking at this card: multitasking, trying to do too many things at once, flexibility, ups and downs, learning how to go with the flow, the dunce, or getting overwhelmed.

The reversed Two of Cups shows the balance is lost. You're dropping the ball. Giving up. It could also mean a decision is made for you. The power is no longer in your hands. You've been demoted. Hard adjusting to changing circumstances. Regretful purchases. The budget is blown, and suddenly you're underwater financially. Stupidity.

How to embody the energy of this card: Take a moment to study the card. When have you committed to too many things? The Two of Pentacles shows up every time you've taken on more responsibilities than you can handle. In that case, you must delegate or decide what your priorities may be. Look for the ways you might be able to streamline your work. Say no to a few things. Then breathe a sigh of relief when you find your balance again.

A question to ponder: *How do you juggle your responsibilities? Do you really need to do it all?*

Tarotcise

 Many cards in the tarot deck speak of choices, not just the Twos. Which other cards may indicate a decision that needs to be made?

The Three of Pentacles

Element: Earth

Three people come together in a temple to work. One pauses with a tool while the other two go over plans. The Three of Pentacles is the card of talent, skilled labor, and teamwork. Collaboration yields beautiful results. Hidden talent or latent skills. Receiving attention for a job well done. You're building something you'll be proud of. Creating a solid foundation for the future. Apprenticeship. Learning on the job. Perfectionism. Spiritual work.

In some cases, this card can mean home improvement projects or the construction of a home.

Other ways of looking at this card: baptism, religious rites, wedding planning, needing to be told what to do, following orders, and productivity.

Let's turn it upside down! The Three of Pentacles reversed can mean shoddy workmanship. An inability to work well with others. A team that can't quite get it together. Sabotage. Poor leadership. Quarrels on the job. No one can agree on anything. Lack of cooperation. As you can imagine, this is the type of opposition that means little gets done . . . or done well.

How to embody the energy of this card: Look for the way teamwork shows up in your life. At work, at home, how do you play well with others? How do jobs get done better with a team? Make an effort to cooperate with coworkers, and see how that creates a productive vibe. Another great way to capture the feeling of the Three of Pentacles: spend time in a house of worship. Look at the beauty around you. Imagine the amount of effort it took to create this sacred space.

A question to ponder: *How can you perfect your skills?*

Tarotcise

Once again, look for the cards that show a church setting. Arrange those cards in different positions. What stories might they be telling about a church? For example, the Three of Pentacles and the Hierophant might be talking about building a new room in the Vatican, while the Four of Swords and Hierophant might indicate the death of a pope.

The Four of Pentacles

Element: Earth

The Four of Pentacles represents stability. Finances are secure as a rock. You've got everything under control. This could be a time when you're feeling on top of your financial game. Or perhaps other things in your life are going well. Whatever the case may be, you're solid gold, baby.

In some cases, this card can also point to miserliness or greed. If that is the case, what can you do to loosen your purse strings?

Other ways of looking at this card: possessiveness, avarice, control freak, staking a claim, graspiness, materialism, or city life.

What about reversed? In that case, the Four of Pentacles suggests letting go of control. Relaxing your grip. Spending money or being generous with others. In some cases, this reversal can indicate financial insecurity. You didn't plan for the future, and now you're freaking out. Scarcity mentality. Coveting other people's money or success. Envy. Using money to control others. Embezzling.

How to embody the energy of this card: Think of something you'd like to purchase in the future. Create a savings plan and begin putting the money aside. Stick to the budget, no matter how tempted you may be to spend that dough. Every time you feel tempted to blow your wad, pull out this card as a reminder to leave your money be.

A question to ponder: *What makes you feel secure?*

Tarotcise

Besides the number 4, what other things do the Four of Pentacles and the Emperor share? Journal your findings.

The Five of Pentacles

Element: Earth

The two figures in the Five of Pentacles sure look misera-
ble. They're broke, injured, and out in the cold. Can you
think of a more uncomfortable position to be in? This card
symbolizes hardship. Financial woes. A period of loss. That
time when you lose your job or home. Insecurity. Home-
lessness. Beggars. But look around you. The stained-glass
window shows help is available. Can you see it? Or are you
choosing to trudge on, unable to spot the help . . . or ask for
it? In some cases, this could be the couple who sticks together through thick
and thin.

The bell on the second figure's neck represents the bells that were put
on lepers to warn others of their presence. The Five of Pentacles can indicate
outsiders. Marginalized folks. People who don't fit in. Shunning. Being ostra-
cized. Illness. Injury.

Other ways of looking at this card: winter, refugees, addicts, poverty, exile, physical hardship, or codependence.

The reversed Five of Pentacles says help is found or accepted. You're
coming in from the cold. Troubles cease, and there is a light at the end of a
long, hard road. Recuperation. Financial aid. Finding shelter.

How to embody the energy of this card: Think of a time when you experienced
financial hardship. Did you ask for help? Or tough it out alone? If you've ever
spent time helping out the needy, you may also understand the vibe of the
Five of Pentacles. Journal what it feels like to need help . . . and give it.

A question to ponder: *How can you ask for help?*

Tarotcise

The Five of Pentacles is one of the cards I use for timing. The snow points to wintertime. This means in a question about timing, we'd be looking at winter. Go through the deck and find other cards with the four seasons. Can you find symbols for each season?

The Six of Pentacles

Element: Earth

On the Six of Pentacles, two beggars sit at the feet of a wealthy merchant who is doling out coins. This card indicates generosity, charity, and financial balance. It can also mean a time when the balance of power is off. One person has more than the other or is in a superior position. Depending on the question, you could be the one holding all the coins or the one begging for help.

In romance, the Six of Pentacles can suggest one person is giving more to the relationship than the other. In other situations, this card can indicate gratitude. If you're offering help or in a position to provide, be grateful.

This could also mean you need help. Don't be too proud to ask.

Other ways of looking at this card: humility, sharing, teaching, sponsor, mentor, bankruptcy, fairness, dominance, or submission.

The reversed Six of Pentacles says that aid is denied. You're turned away into the cold. Greed takes hold, creating a miserly situation. It's also possible that you may feel unable to ask for help. In some cases, this reversal can mean financial woes or legal problems. A situation where one person controls the purse strings and uses it to control another.

How to embody the energy of this card: Give money to a charitable cause. Or do something generous such as help a friend move. To give is divine . . . and an easy way to feel the energy of the Six of Pentacles.

A question to ponder: *Do you give as much as you get?*

Tarotcise

Scrutinize the Six of Pentacles. Notice that the merchant is giving coins to one beggar but not the other. Why is that? Is he ignoring the other person? Is it not their turn? What do you think this might indicate, if anything? Journal your thoughts.

The Seven of Pentacles

Element: Earth

The seeds were planted long ago. The hard work has been done. The Seven of Pentacles says the rewards are beginning to show. This marks a time when you must be patient. After all, a watched pot never boils. It can be difficult to wait, but do know that there are good things ahead for you. Everything that you've done will bear sweet fruit in due time.

In some cases, this card may indicate stepping back and examining your handiwork. How are things coming along? Do you need to weed out anything? Or are you satisfied with your growth? Analyze the situation and revise your plans if need be.

This card can also mean a rest before heading back to work. Take a breather, and then get back on it. There is more that needs to be done. Slow progress. The growth that happens with continuous effort.

Other ways of looking at this card: rethinking, research, pondering, contemplation, assessing the situation, or hardship.

A reversal suggests that nothing is growing. You're going nowhere fast. Wasted efforts. Hard labor. A lot of work with zero rewards. The Seven of Pentacles reversed is the job that doesn't pay well. Financial troubles prevent you from growing your situation or leaving it. A poor investment. The qualities of impatience and laziness are also possible interpretations.

How to embody the energy of this card: Look at where you've worked hard. What results can you see from your good efforts? Journal your thoughts. Another way to embody this card is to plant a garden. Hard work and patience are always involved in gardening. The perfect way to feel the Seven of Pentacles!

A question to ponder: *What is growing right now?*

Tarotcise

Seven is considered a number of challenge. What is the difficulty in this card? How does this compare to the issues that other Sevens might be facing?

The Eight of Pentacles

Element: Earth

The figure in the Eight of Pentacles is focused on his work and making tremendous progress. This is the card of productivity, gainful employment, and enjoyment in one's work. It's also considered to be the card of the intern—a person who gains excellent proficiency in work through doing a job. The desire to learn to get to the next level.

Financially, this card shows steady growth and rewards for a job well done. Pride in work. Accomplishment. All deals are getting hammered out. Working through the issues to fabulous solutions.

Other ways of looking at this card: attention to details, school, apprentice, artisan, dedication, effort.

When this card is reversed, we see poor workmanship. Lazy efforts. Lack of skill. Someone who doesn't pay attention to the little things. Shirking a job. Lack of interest in the current task at hand or distraction. Working for peanuts. Giving up. Dissatisfaction with your position or schooling. Bored out of your gourd at work or school. The student who has potential but squanders it through foolishness.

How to embody the energy of this card: Find a task that needs to be done, such as washing the dishes. Cut out your distractions. Focus only on the job that needs to be done. Notice how quickly and well you get things done when you keep your distractions to a minimum.

A question to ponder: *If you could develop any skill in the world, what would that be?*

Tarotcise

Put the Pentacles suit from Five to Ten in a row. Write a rags-to-riches short story using these cards as prompts.

The Nine of Pentacles

Element: Earth

The Nine of Pentacles symbolizes wealth, prosperity, and living the good life. All the hard work has paid off. Now you can collect the fruits that are blossoming. A period of growth leads to ease. Financial comfort is at hand. You're self-reliant and don't need anyone else's help. You have everything you could possibly want. You made the dream happen! Yay!

But there is also an element of boredom here. Sure, you've got it all, but maybe something is missing. If so, what could that be? What do you still want to grow in your life?

Other ways of looking at this card: garden parties, isolation, boundaries, control, beauty, treating yourself, enjoying the good things that life has to offer, a wealthy person cut off from others, gated communities.

What about when you reverse the Nine of Pentacles? Now you feel trapped. Alone. You cannot see a way out. You may want to be free, but something or someone has you penned in. This reversal can also mean financial issues due to extravagance. Do you really need that bling? Or it may mean an inability to appreciate all that you've been given. The Poor Little Rich Girl. All the money in the world can't buy happiness.

How to embody the energy of this card: Take time to appreciate all the gifts you have around you right now. Give thanks for the blessings you have. Look back and notice what needed to happen to get you here. You've come a long way, baby!

A question to ponder: *What can you appreciate right now?*

Tarotcise

The Empress and woman on the Nine of Pentacles wear similar gowns. What other things do they have in common?

The Ten of Pentacles

Element: Earth

The Ten of Pentacles is the card of legacy. You've worked hard to provide, and now everyone is secure. A time of wealth and prosperity. Total security. A beautiful home. Inheritance. Wills. Winning money. All the good stuff!

This card can also symbolize gathering the family to celebrate some event. This may be a family reunion. In some cases, this card may represent taking care of the ones you love. Everyone living together under the same roof. Honoring family traditions.

Other ways of looking at this card: affluence, magic, community, patriarch, parties, elders, stability, windfall, protection, and family life.

When you reverse the Ten of Pentacles, the harmony is gone. Now you get family drama. Perhaps you're fighting over money. Someone didn't sign the will, and now it's going to probate. An outsider tries to return. The prodigal son or father. A deadbeat who abandons his family and shows up only when there is something to gain. Financial drama. Squandering the family inheritance. Major losses. Gambling everything away. An expensive divorce.

How to embody the energy of this card: Hold a family reunion. Catch up with folks you haven't seen in a while. Spend time with elders and children. Make a point to ensure everyone feels cared for and well fed. Another Ten of Pentacles activity: get the folks together and create a family tree. Who's in your branches?

A question to ponder: *How do you care for your family?*

Tarotcise

In *78 Degrees of Wisdom*, Rachel Pollack points out that the Pentacles in this card form the Tree of Life. She suggests that other cards have a hidden Tree of Life. One of these is indicated in her book *The New Tarot Handbook* (I'm not telling you the secret; you have to look for it!). Find the Tree of Life in other cards.

PAGE of PENTACLES

The Page of Pentacles

Element: Earth

An apt pupil or perfect student, the Page of Pentacles never loses focus. He's fascinated with his studies and sure to bring home honors. This card can represent a young person who makes the grade. The prodigy. This kid is going places!

This card can also indicate good news about money. That can be an investment that pays off, a raise, a loan that comes through when you need it most, or a great money-making idea. You get the job or promotion. Or it can mean a new opportunity that has the potential to be lucrative. This card can advise about starting a new financial plan or a side hustle.

Other ways of looking at this card: practicality, focus, making dreams real, proving yourself, planting seeds for the future, and giving credit where credit is due.

The reversed Page of Pentacles can warn that a lack of focus spells future failure. It can also represent the student who is distracted and never bothers to study for exams. In some cases, it could mean learning disabilities. This can also indicate bad financial news. Something goes belly up. Losing a job or getting laid off. Financial loss because you're not paying attention. A person with poor values or a greedy streak.

How to embody the energy of this card: What fascinates you? Find a hobby or skill that you're obsessed with and commit to learning it.

A question to ponder: *What news would you like to receive at this time?*

Tarotcise

Four Pages can indicate school or a group of children. Take all the Pages out of the deck. What might be their academic interests or talents? For example, is the Page of Pentacles the math whiz, or is she involved in 4H? Journal your thoughts.

The Knight of Pentacles

Element: Earth

Slow and steady wins the race. You've already laid the groundwork. Now you can plant your seeds for the future. Take action on your goals and bit by bit, you'll get there. The Knight of Pentacles is the only Knight who is not moving. He's steady and calm. That may be the energy you need at this moment. Take your time.

This card can also indicate a person who is there when you need them the most. You can count on them every time. They can be stubborn, but at least you know where you stand with them. This reliable Roger will never let you down!

Other ways of looking at this card: hard work, a cautious approach, conservative, dedication, digging in your heels, dogged pursuit of a goal, and a substantial investment of time or money.

The reversed Knight of Pentacles is the person who doesn't take action on their dreams. Instead, they sit around and wait for an opportunity to show up . . . or for someone else to do the work. Laziness. Someone who refuses to do their part. A stubborn, materialistic person who is hell-bent on doing things their way, even if it doesn't produce good results. The micromanager. This card can also indicate a situation in which you do your best, but the circumstances lead to nothing at all, despite all the effort.

How to embody the energy of this card: Set a goal—one that takes time. Then stay on it until the goal is complete. That's how the Knight of Pentacles operates in the world!

A question to ponder: *What makes you feel secure?*

Tarotcise

Notice that the Page of Pentacles stands in a green field, a sign of possibility. Here, the Knight is in a plowed field. What does that signify? What is he trying to grow? Why is he the only Knight not in motion? Ponder these questions and journal your answers.

The Queen of Pentacles

Element: Earth

QUEEN of PENTACLES

The Queen of Pentacles symbolizes the nurturing person who always has a shoulder to lean on and a dollar to lend, taking care of those in need. This Queen knows how to turn a buck into a fortune. She's thrifty, shrewd, and can run a business. She's fertile and creative. These are qualities that you may possess or need. Or this card can represent someone who does.

The Queen of Pentacles can also indicate pregnancy, birth, or home life. Her down-to-earth style means that she is resourceful and always able to make ends meet. You can count on her when the chips are down!

Other ways of looking at this card: service, resources, growth, abundance, trust, creating a nest, pets, caretaking, warmth, generosity, or manifesting.

If you reverse this Queen, she loses her warmth and becomes a person who cannot take care of others or herself. A slob. A selfish, envious person who is only concerned with the bottom line. What's in it for me? In some cases, it can be a helicopter parent—the type who controls their children. A shrew. Henpecking. Nothing is good enough, and no one measures up. Materialism gone amok. The trophy wife. Sometimes this can represent a person stuck in a marriage because they don't have the means to leave on their own. Financial dependence on another person. Infertility or lack of maternal vibe.

How to embody the energy of this card: Spend time taking care of your home. Tidy things up. Make a good meal. Invite friends or family over for dinner. When everyone feels well fed and begins pushing away from the table, gushing over the meal, you've become the Queen of Pentacles.

A question to ponder: *What do you want to manifest?*

Tarotcise

The Queen of Pentacles is a good steward of the earth. In what ways do you see that embodied in this card? How is she taking care of the earth? If she were an environmentalist, what would she be doing right now? Write down your thoughts.

The King of Pentacles

Element: Earth

KING ᴏꜰ PENTACLES.

I always call the King of Pentacles my "King Midas." All the evidence of his hard work is around him. He's built up a secure life, and prosperity encircles him. He wears armor under his suit, a symbol of protection. He is productive, successful, and a master at manifesting. What he focuses on becomes a reality. Protector of the realm, he ensures that everyone around him is safe and well fed. His touch is truly golden.

This card can symbolize you at this time or a person who provides high-level support when you need it most. The could be the generous boss or wealthy patron. The mentor who gives you everything you need to succeed. A father figure who takes care of his brood.

Other ways of looking at this card: affluence, security, CEO, leader, generosity, and the good life.

The reversed King of Pentacles is the deadbeat. The person who lives beyond their means or who cannot provide for their family. A control freak who uses money as a weapon. Someone who flaunts their wealth. A corrupt politician or CEO who pillages the land for gain. In some cases, this could be a white-collar criminal—a person who embezzles from their company.

How to embody the energy of this card: Kings are masters, and the King of Pentacles is the master of the coin. If you're responsible with money, you've got his vibe down. If you're not, spend time with a financial advisor. How might an advisor guide you to becoming more like this character?

A question to ponder: *What would it take to manifest your financial goals?*

Tarotcise

 Notice that the King's foot is on a stone carving. What does that mean? Like the Emperor, he wears armor under his gown. How does that connect these two?

Alrighty, peeps. We've made it to the end of the tarot meanings part. Take a deep breath. It's a lot to digest.

You might find yourself wondering: how on earth will I remember all of this? Good news: you don't have to. Whew!

When you first begin reading tarot, you may assume that you have to get all those interpretations memorized. *Nope.* As you continue to practice, you'll start to get some of those meanings hammered into your skull, but I want to remind you: it's not necessary. In fact, these are only guidelines—prompts for you to fall back on when your intuition stalls.

So please learn the standard meanings, but don't get hung up on them. Also, as you grow and develop your tarot practice, you'll find new ways of looking at the cards, ways that are unique to you. Perhaps you'll find interpretations that no one else has yet discovered. After all, the cards may have been around for a long time, but your tarot voice offers a fresh perspective.

PART TWO

Intuition Basics

Huh?

When I was a little girl, I remember that moment when my mother shuffled to the door, opened it wide, and slammed it shut. No one was there. None of us heard the doorbell ring—just her. As she whirled around, eyes bulging and mouth pulled into a tight, thin line, she declared, "Someone is going die."

Sure enough, a few days later, we were heading out to a funeral.

This story may sound strange to folks who don't believe in supernatural stuff. But my mom was raised by an Irish mother who believed in banshees, ghosts, and dreams. Plus, they were dirt-poor farm folk, so following their instincts meant survival.

My father's mother was superstitious too, but in a different way. A devout Catholic, she was always burning candles for this saint or that one. When a tornado hit, she hustled us down to the tiny root cellar, little torches in hand, praying for a miracle. After the storm passed, she credited her prayers as the reason we were spared.

This environment impacted me down to the marrow. Candles and rituals were part of my daily life. But so were those omens.

My mother's visions were not always dramatic, however. For example, one day, she had a "funny feeling" about kangaroos. Later that night on the news, a reporter was talking about an escaped kangaroo. How did my mother pick up on such a random thing? It's intuition.

What Is Intuition Exactly?

The online *Merriam-Webster* dictionary defines *intuition* like this:

- A natural ability or power that makes it possible to know something without any proof or evidence; a feeling that guides a person to act a certain way without fully understanding why.

In other words, it's that weird sensation where you understand something immediately, without any facts, logic, or reasoning. You don't know why you're getting that vibe, but you can't ignore it. It's the animal instinct, the gut feeling, the aha moment, or that ability to size up a situation from feeling rather than conscious thinking.

Let me give you a few examples:

Example #1: Warning flag.

You start dating a new guy, and you have a gut feeling that something is "off" about him. You can't explain what, exactly, but you decide to steer clear. Later, you find out that—gulp—he's a compulsive gambler who stole hundreds of thousands of dollars from his elderly mother. (Your intuition warned you about this guy, and it was spot-on!)

Example #2: Gentle nudge.

You meet someone at a party, and you can't shake this feeling that you "know" them already. You're immediately drawn to them. You chat for only a few minutes, and yet your gut keeps telling you, "Don't let this person slip away. Send them an email. Keep in touch." Then you become lifelong friends or even romantic partners. (Your intuition was gently nudging you to follow up and begin a relationship.)

Example #3: Sudden urge.

You're walking your dog, and you see a candy bar wrapper on the ground. It's a Twix bar. You suddenly think to yourself, "That's my friend Sally's all-time favorite candy bar!" For reasons unknown, you feel a strong urge to call Sally right that second, just to say "Hi." She answers and says, "OMG, I was just thinking about you too! I have so much news to tell you. . . " (Your intuition gave you that urge to reach out!)

Example #4: Gut instinct.

You run a business, and you need to hire a new staff member. You interview two people. The first person has all the right credentials and, on paper, he seems like the perfect fit. The second person doesn't really have the exact training you were looking for, but for some reason, you have a gut feeling that she's the right person to hire. You trust your gut and give her the job. Turns out, not only is she a quick learner and a hard worker, but her personality is so upbeat and infectious that every single person at your company feels happier coming to work. Productivity goes up. Sales go up. Morale goes up. (All because you trusted that gut feeling and chose her over the more logical choice.)

Example #5: Deeper wisdom.

You go to the doctor because you've got a funny bump on your neck. She checks you out and says that it's just a slightly swollen lymph node—very common, it happens sometimes, it's really nothing to worry about. You go to another specialist and get a second opinion. You're told the same thing. Yet, you just can't shake the feeling that something isn't right. You go see a third specialist and—yikes—turns out you were right! That bump has got to be removed right away. (Your intuition was guiding you in the right direction, even though several experts missed the signals that you were sensing.)

You've probably had plenty of experiences similar to the ones I just mentioned. Or maybe you've heard other people talk about situations like those. Maybe you have intuitive experiences every day, or perhaps for you, it's not quite that frequent.

Sadly, in contemporary Western cultures, we're often taught to ignore our intuition because it's not "logical" or "rational" and "doesn't make sense." But in my opinion, that's tragic because your intuition can be very wise and often, very, very accurate. Sometimes annoyingly precise. (If you've ever had an experience where your intuition told you something, but you ignored the message and then regretted it later . . . you know what I'm talking about!)

So how does tarot factor into all of this?

Simple: doing tarot is an awesome intuition-booster!

You can use your tarot deck as a tool to wake up your intuition, dust off those cobwebs, and strengthen your intuitive muscles. Doing a tarot reading is like weight lifting for your intuition. The more you exercise, the stronger it gets!

What happens once your intuition becomes stronger?

Answer: really good things.

I've had so many people say to me, "Once I started doing tarot readings regularly, it's like my intuition went from 'sleep mode' to 'fully activated.' I started getting powerful gut instincts all throughout my day—at home, at work, with my kids—and those instincts were usually spot-on!"

Whether you call it "intuition" or "hunches" or "gut instincts" or "signs from the Universe," there's no doubt about it: tarot can help you to tune in to information that's not entirely logical and yet still very useful.

I've been doing tarot readings for close to forty years as of this writing. When I first started, although I trusted my intuition, I still had moments when my confidence wasn't there. My sixth sense felt like a tiny little whisper. Sometimes I could hear it clearly, and other times, the voice was very faint and hard to decipher. But as the years rolled on—through practicing tarot—I could feel my intuition growing stronger, deeper, and louder. Instead of just a teensy little whisper, it became a steady, confident voice. This has been an excellent thing for me, and it has saved my ass on more than one occasion! Like that one time an attractive guy was flirting hard with me, but my intuition kept saying, *"Stay away!"* Later I found out he was convicted of a violent and gruesome murder (it was actually a famous front-page case!). Holy crap! Thanks, intuition. I really dodged a bullet. Literally. (More on him in a second . . .)

Intuition isn't always profound or spooky. Sometimes it's arbitrary and downright silly—like the time I was sitting in my office when suddenly I got my own vision of socks embroidered with monkeys. As I poured myself a cup of tea, I said to my husband, "Someone is going to give me a pair of monkey socks." He laughed.

A few months later, long after I had forgotten about this conversation, a client sat down at the tarot table and said, "Oh, I have a gift for you." She pulled out a pair of monkey socks. I was stunned. There is no way she could have known about my silly prediction because the only person I told was my husband. Of course, I ran upstairs to show him the prize. Needless to say, he was impressed. (I think he would have been more dazzled if I were able to predict lottery numbers!)

The Clairs

I would be remiss to talk about intuition without discussing the different types of intuitive abilities, also called "clairs." These are the top three:

Clairvoyant
Clairaudient
Clairsentient

Clairvoyant means the ability to "see" things that are not perceptible to the naked eye. A person may see auras or get a vision or picture in their mind, which may be prophetic.

Clairaudient is the ability to hear things beyond the reach of natural hearing—often a sound, song, word, sentence, or voice from the dead. No, it's not like hearing voices in your head, silly! But it may be that you hear something that no one else does, and it may be an important message.

Clairsentient means "feeling" something such as a kick in the gut or the hair standing up on the back of your neck. Although I use the other clairs, I am incredibly clairsentient. Here's an example of how it works for me: Years ago, my mother was in the hospital for an extended visit. She had always been a sickly woman, so it wasn't an uncommon thing. But this time, her stay was longer than usual. The doctors didn't give us many answers as to what was wrong with her, but something was definitely up. Finally, I got one on the phone who gently informed me that my mother was gravely ill and "had about a year to live."

Relieved that I had an answer, I thought I could at least get to work organizing things and making sure my ninety-year-old father would have support. Later that night, I was taking one of my nightly strolls with my husband. It was a gorgeous evening with a midnight blue sky dotted with silvery stars. As we were walking, I became aware of a strange sensation. It felt like someone was sawing away at where my umbilical cord would be. "She doesn't have a year to live. She's dying now," I told my husband.

My mother had a stroke in the middle of the night and passed away a few days later. Because I'm that physically sensitive, I could feel the energy. Most people might ignore something like that or brush it off as a ticklish tummy. But I knew it was a sign.

Another dramatic example is my encounter with the murderous dude. Years ago, when I was a bright young thing enjoying a stint in New York City, a hippieish guy was chasing me around the park, trying to get my number. He was totally my type—long, gorgeous hair, great smile, and a razor-sharp wit. This has always been the key to my heart. We were enjoying some playful flirting when I suddenly got a feeling like a shudder up my spine. Something was off. I couldn't put my finger on it, but I knew this wasn't someone I should date. So I gently declined his offer of a date, and we became friends instead. A year later, he was front-page news, charged with the horrific murder of his dancer girlfriend.

My sixth sense kept me safe!

Think to some of the times when you've had a funny feeling or heard some random word outta nowhere. Did you ignore it? If so, did you later look back on that situation and wish you had paid attention? Or, did you trust that vibe? If you did, you were probably glad you didn't ignore it. And, if you were in a similar situation as mine with the murderous hippie, you might be relieved you are still here today.

I'd also like to mention that for many people, the dream world is where their intuition can really get to work. Why? It's because our rational mind is at rest, giving our subconscious full rein to do its thing! Dreams are often rich in symbols, and like the tarot, those symbols hold meanings. They might clue you into a situation that needs your attention . . . or some deep inner work that is happening in your subconscious. In some cases, these dreams can be prophetic.

For example, a dream about a deceased loved one might be helping you through the grieving process, or it may be a message for the living. A few years ago, my children's paternal grandfather passed away. I did not have a relationship with this man because I had divorced his son many years earlier. In the dream, he was sitting on a lawn chair in a beautiful garden, wearing a red flannel shirt, and smoking a cigarette with a cocktail in hand (that was typical of him in real life!). As I approached him, I noticed how good he looked. I asked him how he was, and he said, "I'm great. I love my new home! Tell the kids to sell the house." I woke up and wrote down the dream. At this time, the family home had been sitting for a few years. His son was in no hurry to sell it and had been dawdling with the process. I gave my daughter the message and urged her to tell her uncle what his father had said. She shook her head and said, "He doesn't believe in any of that stuff." Two weeks later, her uncle called to let her know that he had sold the house. The dream was a sign that the grandfather was letting go, and soon the family would be too.

Of course, you'll want to use your journal to record not only tarot readings but also dreams like this or other intuitive hits you may receive.

When you journal, it's crucial to pay close attention to which of the clairs is operating for you. You might find that all three seem to be firing on full cylinders. Or perhaps one appears to be dominant. Maybe it's a dream that came true. Write down all those random feelings, messages, and insights, even if they seem like so much nonsense. Keeping track will help you understand which of your intuitive faculties is your strength . . . or not.

So What Is "Intuitive Tarot Reading" and How Does It Work?

When you're doing "intuitive tarot reading," it means you're relying on your intuition—not the guidebook or manual that came with your tarot deck—to interpret the cards lying in front of you.

For example, say you shuffle your deck and pull out the card that's called the Nine of Pentacles.

Looking at this card, what's your gut instinct about what it means? (Don't Google it or rush to look up the answer in the interpretation section. Let your intuition speak to you instead.)

What do you think this card is trying to tell you?

When you look at the various images—the grapes, the bird, the woman, the coins—what emotions come up for you?

Right away, your eye might be drawn to the woman wearing the luxurious robe, surrounded by gold coins, and you might think to yourself: "I'm allowed to enjoy the wealth that I've worked hard to create. That's what this card is trying to tell me."

Or your eye might be drawn to the tiny little snail on the ground, and you might think to yourself: "It's time to slow down. I should go ahead and book that vacation I've been thinking about. I've earned it!"

Or maybe you notice the little house way in the background of the card and think to yourself: "Hmm. Maybe I've gotten so obsessed with earning money lately that I've wandered away from my 'home.' Maybe it's time to devote a bit more time to my family."

You could pull this exact same card—the Nine of Pentacles—and you could stare at that same card every day for a week. And each day, you might have a subtly (or dramatically) different response to the card's imagery, depending on your state of mind and what's going on in your life that day.

The reason is that each day your subconscious (or intuitive) mind is processing new information and contemplating different questions, so each day your interpretation of the card is going to feel a bit different. Of course, the context of your question may also give you a completely different meaning for the card. When you have a specific question, your instincts kick into high gear to search for what that card might have to say.

Why Is It So Awesome to Practice "Intuitive Tarot Reading"?

When you practice intuitive tarot reading, you're flexing your intuitive muscles and helping them to grow stronger. Stronger intuition means that you'll get clearer gut feelings throughout your daily life, and you'll be more likely to trust those feelings instead of ignoring them.

Instead of pulling a card and then rushing to go look it up in a tarot manual to find out what it's supposed to mean, you're asking yourself, "What do I think this means? What's the specific message for me?"

When you turn inward—and allow your intuition to respond to the card—you're strengthening that part of your brain.

When you turn outward—and rely on the definition that's given to you in a manual—that's not really helping to hone your intuition.

But Seriously, Is It Bad to Rely on a Tarot Manual or Guidebook?

As I said before, relying on a tarot manual or guidebook is not bad, but I wouldn't recommend doing it long term. Again, the interpretation section in this manual is only a guideline to get you acquainted with the meanings. You don't want to keep leaning on them.

Think of it this way: When you're a little kid and you're just learning how to swim, your mom might put one of those inflatable jackets or some water wings on you to help you float. Nothing wrong with that!

Over time, though, as your skill and confidence grow, you don't really need those wings anymore. They're bulky, and they just get in the way. Take 'em off. Now you can swim faster, dive underwater, express yourself with total freedom. You feel more empowered, and you're relying on your own muscles to propel you around the pool instead of an inflatable contraption. So cool!

Same thing with tarot.

When you purchase a brand-new tarot deck, you might want to read the manual that came along with the deck just to familiarize yourself with the cards—their names, what order they appear, the artist's thoughts behind each image, and perhaps some of the general ideas that each card tends to represent. Or maybe you want to flip through a book like this one. That's fine.

I strongly recommend that you eventually put that little white book (and this manual) away and use your intuition—not a book—to interpret the cards. The sooner you do this, the better. Otherwise, if you continue to refer back to your manual every time, you're just going to be regurgitating the messages that are printed inside your manual rather than allowing your intuition to speak to you.

And that's kinda the whole point of doing tarot, right? Waking up your intuition.

So I urge you to get "off book" as soon as you can. Toss that manual aside. You really don't need it. After a while, you'll see that I'm right about that. (Yeah, I'm making a prediction right here, right now!)

This Is Essential

Humans have busy minds. Most people will admit that their brains are in overdrive, churning information, emotions, ideas, and worries constantly. They rarely shut down.

This mental circus gets in the way of hearing that still, small voice within. It's hard to listen to your instincts when you're thinking about last night's date, tomorrow's exam, and that latest reality show episode with the table-tipping screaming match. In fact, getting distracted by all that nonsense is all too easy.

For those who have been working with their intuition for a long time, this sort of thing doesn't seem to get in the way. But for people who are just beginning to work with their sixth sense, all that mental noise may prove to be a problem. Quieting that down is essential.

A quiet mind hears better. Period.

When your mind is not getting slammed with outside interference, it's easier to access your wise self. Your senses are sharper when you have nothing else clamoring for your attention. You might wonder how to find that peaceful mindset. Fortunately, it's not hard. It begins with meditation.

There are a lot of misconceptions around meditation. "It's too hard. I can't sit still. It's boring. I don't know where to start. I tried, but I can't make my mind blank! Am I doing it wrong?"

Relax, Grasshopper. It's not hard.

Let's cover a few of those mistaken beliefs first:

1. Meditation is not difficult. Anyone can do it. It doesn't require any special tools or training. All you are doing is sitting and quieting the mind.

2. If you can't sit still, try sitting for a short time. Or test out walking meditation. It's a fabulous alternative for the fidgety.

3. It's not boring! Constant mental chatter is annoying. A clear mind is expansive and exciting. Finally, you see the possibilities and signs instead of being inundated with the whoop-whoop of the monkey mind!

4. Starting is simple. Just sit where you are. Boom!

5. The goal is not to make your mind blank. Instead, you're sitting and noticing how your brain operates. For example, I'm a planner. When I sit, often my mind drifts into my plans for the day, week, or year. As soon as I catch myself heading into planning mode, I label my thoughts "planning" and then let them go. Doing this helps me understand my thinking processes and, more importantly, it helps me make peace with myself. I often say that meditation is a way to become more compassionate toward yourself. With regular meditation practice, you can make friends with your mind, and that allows you to show up as your best self in the world.

6. There is no right or wrong way to meditate.

I regularly use a few meditations: simple breath work, loving-kindness meditation (also called metta meditation), and chakra opening/closing.

Before we go through each type, here are a few tips to make the most of your meditation practice:

1. Find comfortable seating. As I say to my yoga students: if you're not comfortable, you won't be meditating. You'll only be thinking about how uncomfortable you are. If you like to sit cross-legged on the floor, do so. But you might find that you prefer a cushion under your hips or maybe enjoy sitting on a chair or couch instead. If you use a wheelchair, you can remain seated as you are. For people with bad backs, I recommend sitting with your back against the wall or on a chair with a sturdy back. In some cases, lying on the floor may be best.

2. Be sure that you are warm. Dress in layers or drape a blanket over your body. Being too hot or cold will disrupt your practice.

3. An eye pillow is a great prop if you are lying down. It shuts out light, and the gentle weight relaxes the eyes.

4. Start with short periods. Five minutes is enough. Even if you *only* do five minutes a day for the rest of your life, meditation will help a great deal.

5. You might want to use a timer. Timers with chimes are available, as well as apps you can download on your cell phone.

6. If you have a restless mind, consider downloading a guided meditation. Many good ones are on the market. Research until you find one that you like. I'm a huge fan of hypnosis and have an app on my phone that allows me to choose various hypnosis sessions depending on how I want to feel. (I usually select peace!)

The Meditations

Simple Breath Work: This is the most accessible meditation and the one I use for everyday practice. Sit comfortably, close your eyes, and then choose a place to anchor your awareness. This could be the tip of the nostrils or the rise and fall of your abdomen.

Begin observing your breath as it comes and goes. Do not try to change or control the breathing in any way. Just witness each inhale and exhale as they are. Notice the quality of each breath. Become aware of the little pauses at the top of the inhale and the bottom of each exhale. Pay attention to how different each breath feels.

At some point, your mind may wander. When that happens, notice. Label those thoughts: "Planning. Worrying. Stewing. Daydreaming. Etc." Then direct your attention back to your breath. After a few minutes, begin wiggling your fingers and toes. Stretch a limb or two if you feel that you need to. Open your eyes and come back to the room.

Loving-Kindness Meditation (Metta Meditation): I do this meditation when I'm feeling sad about the world or when I'm dealing with some particularly nasty people. We empathic folk can get quickly drained or depleted from a messy world or a mean comment. This meditation pulls me back into compassion mode immediately. You might be wondering why I include this meditation. It's simple: when we are anchored in the present moment and kindness, our tarot and intuitive work are better. It's hard to hear when you're stuck in the echo chamber of fear.

Sit comfortably and close your eyes. Begin following your breath. As you inhale silently, say to yourself, "May I be free from suffering." On the exhale, "May I be at peace." Repeat this mantra with each breath. Practice for a few minutes.

You can direct the mantra toward a hater if you find that they are pulling you off-center. In this case, you would replace *I* with the name of the problematic person. For example: "May Essie be free from suffering. May Essie be at peace." By sending this good energy to them, you're breaking the negative connection between you. More importantly, you're sending that person much-needed compassion. Because even negative types need that—probably more so than most people.

I often use this meditation for clients who are in pain too. After a tarot session, I sit quietly for a few minutes and send these positive affirmations while visualizing the client. In my opinion, this is another way to serve the people who come to me for readings.

Open the Chakras: This is the meditation I use before I begin my work with the tarot. It's perfect for opening the psychic channels! If you don't know what chakras are, they are energy centers in the body. There are many chakras, but the primary seven are what I work with: Root, Navel, Solar Plexus, Heart, Throat, Third Eye, and Crown. Each chakra has a color associated with it: red, orange, yellow, green, blue, indigo, and violet. For this meditation, I use a flower opening image to open the chakras.

Sit in a comfortable position and close your eyes. Begin to engage in abdominal breathing. Let your breath come and go with ease. When you feel calm, direct your attention to your tailbone. This is where your Root chakra resides. Visualize a bright red flower at the base of your spine. As you breathe in, see the flower opening its petals wide. Take a few more breaths and then move up to your Navel chakra, which is an inch or two below your navel. In your mind's eye, see a brilliant orange flower and then breathe into that flower, opening the petals all the way. When you feel ready to move on, direct your attention to your Solar Plexus area, which is right above your belly button. Here find a sunny yellow flower and breathe into it. Once again, witness the petals opening up, revealing the different shades of yellow at the center of the flower.

Bring your awareness to the Heart chakra, which is located directly underneath your sternum. Visualize an emerald green flower and take a deep breath. As you exhale, watch the petals of the green flower opening up and spreading across your sternum. Rest here for a few breaths and then move on. At the Throat chakra, picture a vivid blue flower. Breathe into it and watch the petals unfold. Take a moment and then move up to the Third Eye, which is right between the eyebrows. Take a few breaths here and then see an indigo flower, bright and luminous, and breathe into it. The petals open, revealing a center that looks like a sapphire. Rest here for a few breaths and then move to the Crown chakra, which is located at the top of the head. Breathe in and out for a moment and then visualize a violet lotus flower at the top of your crown. As you breathe into it, a thousand petals spread wide open. Remain here for a few moments. When you feel ready, open your eyes.

You're ready to connect with your inner guidance . . . and your tarot.

Close the Chakras: At the end of the day, I make sure to close down the chakras. This meditation helps protect my energy, and it prevents me from absorbing every vibe in the Universe. Yes, that can and does happen. That's because intuitive people tend to pick up on energy too easily. This leads to weak boundaries. As I often say, those weak boundaries are what makes us good at this work, but it's also what gets us into trouble. Protecting your energy field is a vital skill that every intuitive tarot reader should develop. This meditation is quick and does the trick nicely.

Once again, sit quietly with your eyes closed. Take a few slow, deep breaths. Then bring your awareness to the Crown chakra. Breathe in and out for a moment and then visualize the violet lotus flower closing its petals tightly. When you feel ready, move on to the Third Eye. Picture the indigo flower in your mind and then slowly close the petals. Take your attention to the Throat chakra. Once again, visualize the blue flower at the throat. Take in a breath and then close the flower tightly. Next, move down to the Heart chakra. Breathe into the green flower and then shut the petals. Remain here for a few more breaths and then move on. Rest your attention at the Solar Plexus chakra for a moment. Visualize the yellow flower and then gently shut the petals. Move your awareness down to the Navel chakra, where the orange flower rests. Take in a nice deep breath and then close the orange flower until it's nice and tight. Finally, move on to the Root chakra. Breathe in and out for a few moments. Then close the red flower all the way until it's securely shut. Once again, remain here for a few moments. When you feel centered and protected, open your eyes.

These are the meditations I use the most. There are others I like, but for intuitive work, these four are useful . . . and all you need.

Om-work!

Begin working with these meditations immediately. Test them out. See how they make you feel. Practice a few minutes every day. For extra shazam, keep your journal handy and make notes of any insights that might arise during your meditation.

One of the beautiful things that happens for me during meditation is my creativity kicks in. Some of my most significant and best ideas come during my meditation sessions! It's also a time when vital intuitive hits seem to happen effortlessly. Blank mind? Not here. My brain adores meditation, and yours will too.

Intuition Buzzkills

While I believe that we all possess intuition, some situations and mindsets can get in the way and muddy the psychic waters.

Here are a few intuition buzzkills that may hinder your ability to tap in and trust your sixth sense:

Skepticism: Have you ever encountered a skeptic? You know the type: they don't believe that "woo-woo stuff" and will dismiss it completely or try to find some scientific reason to debunk it. While there is nothing wrong with a healthy dose of skepticism, too much of it and you become a cynic. When that happens, you'll be a doubting Thomas, even when the writing is clearly on the wall . . . or in the cards. This is why journaling is so crucial. If you tend to lean toward the skeptic mindset, keeping track of your readings and intuitive hits might help you see that it's working just fine.

If you're a skeptic, I recommend reading *The Gift of Fear and Other Survival Signals That Protect Us from Violence* by Gavin de Becker. This book talks about how many victims of violence often feel a sense that something is wrong, and in some cases, they ignore that feeling . . . only to regret it later. I often think about the time I avoided that killer hippie. Imagine if I had let my skeptical side get in the way! I might not be here writing this book today.

The fear of being wrong: Next to skepticism, the fear of getting it wrong is the strongest psychic muzzle. Look, you're not always going to be right every single time. No one has that ability. Things can (and will) be misinterpreted. It happens to the best of us! Remember that you are only human. Cut yourself some slack, and in those situations where you make a bad call, learn from it. I usually find that my instincts or the cards were correct, but my brain was not picking up on what it meant.

Emotions: Being emotionally invested in an outcome or in a frazzled state will color your sixth sense every time. To get a clear message, you have to get your emotions in a good place so the information can come through without a "feeling filter." I talk more about this in the "Fine-Tuning Your Intuitive Tarot Readings" chapter.

Overly analytical: If you get a hunch but then spend a whole lotta time overanalyzing it, your rational mind will find a way to interfere. Sound like you? The best plan of action is to write down your impressions and leave them be. Do not fret over what they may or may not mean. Instead, come back to them later and see how they worked out.

Substances: While alcohol or drugs can relax the nerves and open the third eye, using them is a dangerous path to tread because they usually lead to cloudy, faulty impressions. If you want to be a clear channel, you may need to forgo the substances. (I *never* drink and mix tarot. *Ever.* Personally, I think it's irresponsible.) Instead, try meditation. It will give you the most reliable connection to your intuition. However, if you are taking medication for a physical or mental health condition, it may actually help you. The reason: if you're not feeling well, that can impact your ability to tune in. My mother struggled with mental illness and was on medication for most of her adult life. If she didn't have that support, her anxiety might have affected her intuitive faculties. In some cases, medication can actually be an ally for calming the nerves, and that can be essential for keeping your mind calm enough to pick up on vibes.

Intuition is a delicate, sensitive instrument. An open mind with a bit of curiosity and trust will keep it sharp and reliable.

What's All This Got to Do with Tarot?

Anybody can learn to read tarot. I'm serious about that. There are standard interpretations and lots of methods you can use. But the really great readers don't just rely on those systems and rote meanings; they let their intuition guide the way.

I like to compare reading tarot to being a musician. If you want, you can learn to play an instrument. With practice, you might even become proficient. But if you don't have rhythm and soul, you will never sound as good as someone who does.

That doesn't mean you need to be a prodigy. Remember, some people don't have a lick of natural ability, but their ambition motivates them to practice, practice, practice. That dedication can take anyone from average to masterful.

It's the same with tarot and intuition. As you practice working with both, you will soon find that the energy begins to flow. Information will seem to spill out of your mind and mouth. As with automatic writing, you won't even have to stop and think. The message will simply come.

Hone Your Intuition

We've discussed what intuition is and isn't. We've covered the basics of keeping a journal and meditation. Now let's work on developing those psychic muscles!

Let's start by warming up. A few simple intuitive stretches first and then some Tarotcises that combine cards and sixth sense! Let the games begin!

Playing cards: For this drill, you'll need a regular playing card deck. Shuffle the cards thoroughly. Then, lay them facedown on the table in front of you. Take the first card in your hand, and without turning it over, focus on what you're feeling. Can you guess which card it might be? Is it the Ace of Hearts? Or the Seven of Clubs? Maybe a King? Turn the card over. Were you right . . . or not? Go through the entire pack, keeping track of which guesses are correct or not. (This is a great game to do with children or when you're bored on the plane. Much better than solitaire!)

Phone home: Whenever the phone rings, take a moment to tune in to who might be calling. No peeking at caller ID! Pick it up and see who's on the line. Did you guess correctly? More phone fun: in the morning, write down the names of anyone you think might call you. It's uncanny, but when I do this, almost 90 percent of the time I will receive a call from that person. One twist on this: I'll put names of clients I haven't heard from in a while. Sure enough, within a few days, I get a call! Telepathy through telephones! Ha!

Picture this: This exercise is best done with a group. Everyone brings pictures of people they know well, but others may not know. Each member will take a minute to study the image and then write down any impressions that they are getting. Those insights can range from notes on the person's personality to something that might be going on in their life. Encourage a "no filter rule": tell folks to simply write down first impressions without stopping to "correct" them. After everyone has had a chance to write down their thoughts, take turns sharing their ideas with the group. The person who brought the picture can confirm which guesses are correct . . . or not.

You can do this exercise on your own by studying people in the news. Notice what you feel about them. Do they feel happy? Cruel? Are you picking up on some event that might be happening in their life? Make notes. A few days or weeks later, do a search on the internet to see if you can find any confirming information.

Gifted: When someone gives you a gift, see if you can guess what it is. Do *not* do this in front of the giver! I'm so good at this that my husband has now resorted to doing things to distract me (which usually involves getting me mad) to throw me off the scent!

Good Morning: At the beginning of the day, write down something random such as "white horse" and then see if it shows up in your life in some way that day.

Cappucin-know: If you're in line at the coffee shop, see if you can guess what the person behind you—or in front of you—will order. It's like being a psychic barista!

Billets: Do you remember the Carnac the Magnificent skit on *The Tonight Show Starring Johnny Carson*? Carson played a mystic in a huge feathered turban who would divine the answer to a question in an envelope. Although the skit was humorous, billets are my all-time favorite intuition exercise, hands down.

A billet (pronounced *bill-ay*) is a slip of paper with a question written on it. The billet is dropped into a bowl or hat and is then drawn randomly. The person who pulls the billet will take a moment to hold it without looking at the question. Instead, that person tunes into the subject and shares any impressions they receive. Next, the billet is opened and the question read. This exercise loosens people up and often freaks people out when they correctly answer a question—which happens more than you might expect.

Billets can also be funny. I was teaching a class in Detroit, and we were using the billets exercise. A volunteer pulled out a billet, sat quietly for a moment, and said, "I feel sick to my stomach. Something is wrong. I'm queasy." She opened the slip of paper, and the question was, "What was Kanye West thinking when he met Donald Trump at the Oval Office?" As you can imagine, this cracked up the whole room.

Another twist on billets is to write down a name instead of a question. The name should be someone who is known by the person writing it down. Or, in some cases, you may want to use the names of celebrities or well-known media figures. Once again, the billet is drawn randomly, and the participant takes a moment to hold it and share impressions. Once this is done, they open the paper and read the name.

Billets are effective in groups of all sizes. It's especially cool when someone picks their own question and answers it. Often this produces some gasps when the participant turns it over and realizes they just answered their own question. And sometimes this gives them just the insight they needed!

I was doing billets with a large group when one man pulled his own question. As he held the note in his hand, the messages "hard work" and "long road to go" came up. He seemed nervous about being wrong and perhaps offending someone else in the room. When he opened the billet, his question was about a new business he was just beginning to pull together. He laughed out loud and said it was true since he had only started with the planning stages.

If you don't have a group to work with, you can still do this solo. Here's how: write down a lot of questions. Perhaps twenty. Fold them up and put them into a bowl. Randomly pick one and, just like above, feel the answer. Then open the billet and see how your insights worked out. I also recommend doing this when you have a bunch of questions that you are having a hard time finding answers to. Your intuition knows what's up. You might discover billets are a fab way for your sixth sense to kick in with the goods when your common sense doesn't want to cooperate.

These little exercises are simple but effective. If you do them often enough, you'll find that you will become more confident in your psychic abilities.

Tarotcise

Now that you're warmed up, let's move on to some heavy lifting with my ten fave Tarotcises to wake up your intuition and get you reading like a boss!

For these exercises, you'll need:

- A tarot deck (any one that you like!)

- A flat surface, like a desk or table

- Some paper or a notebook

- Something to write with

- A little bit of free time (none of these exercises take more than a few minutes)
- An open mind

Tarotcise #1: Simple Meditation

Sit comfortably. Take a cleansing breath. Shuffle your tarot deck.

Ask yourself an open-ended question. Something like:

- "What do I need to know today?"
- "What should I focus on at work today?"
- "What's the best way for me to proceed with [*situation*]?"
- "How can I move toward a successful result with [*project*]"?
- "Why is [*situation*] repeatedly happening in my life? What do I need to learn?"

Select a card. Set the card in front of you. Soften your gaze. Sit quietly for a few minutes, letting your eyes move about the image. What thoughts arise? What symbols catch your attention? What do you feel the card is trying to tell you?

Take your time with this meditation.

After a few minutes, write down any insights that you may have received.

Tarotcise #2: Storytelling

Sit comfortably. Take a cleansing breath. Shuffle your tarot deck.

Ask yourself an open-ended question (see Tarotcise #1 for a few examples).

Select a card. Set the card in front of you. Looking at the image, begin telling a story. (You can do this out loud or by writing the story in your notebook.)

I like to start with, "Once upon a time . . ."

As you continue to spin your tale, notice how it might be related to your question or situation. What does the story tell you about the card? What does the story tell you about yourself?

This Tarotcise is excellent if you're feeling stuck and unable to get anything from the cards. Storytelling can jog your intuition. As you begin narrating a tale inspired by the images, you may receive epiphanies on what the card means in the context of your question.

Tarotcise #3: Automatic Writing

Same preparation as before. Sit. Breathe. Shuffle. Ask a question. Pull a card.

This time, instead of pondering the card's meaning inside your head, and instead of writing a story, just start writing . . . anything. Pen to paper: go! Write automatically without editing or censoring yourself. You can begin with a phrase like "The first thing I noticed was . . . " or "I think this card means . . . " or any other phrase that comes to mind.

Write for a few minutes. Let the words spill out. Don't worry if your writing doesn't seem to make any sense. Let it flow!

When you're done, review what you've written. Any insights? If not, consider revisiting what you've written the following day after sleeping on it. How about now?

Tarotcise #4: Eye-Catcher

Shuffle your deck. This time, fan out the entire deck on your desk or table, faceup, so that you can see all the images.

Let your eyes wander. Do you see a card that seems to jump out or catch your eye? Select that card.

Place that card in front of you. Clear the others away.

Now, look even closer at the card. Closer. *Annnnd* closer. Find one small detail on the card that intrigues you. Perhaps a tiny snail. A single flower. A bird far away in the background. A wrinkle in someone's cloak. Maybe the oar of a boat.

Focus intently on that one specific piece of the image.

What thoughts arise? What do you feel that one little detail is trying to tell you?

Write down any insights that you may have received.

Tarotcise #5: Memento

Did you ever see the movie *Memento*? The film tells the story of a man who is trying to solve the murder of his wife, but he has a rare disorder that creates short-term memory loss, which means he needs to relive the situation backward to piece the whole story together.

You can use what I call the "Memento technique" in your next tarot reading. For this Tarotcise, you'll want to do a multicard spread, like the Celtic Cross.

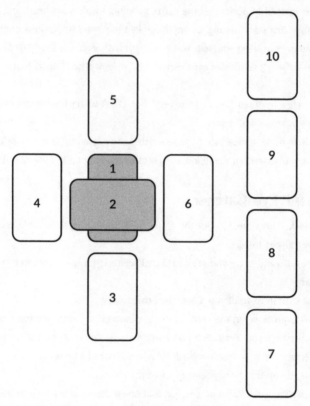

(No idea what I'm talking about? Skip this Tarotcise for now. We'll revisit the Celtic Cross and Memento Tarotcises under "Sample Readings" in the "First Things First" chapter on page 201.)

Starting with the card in the "final outcome" position, interpret backward, card by card, until you come to the first card in the spread. Basically, you're reversing the order in which you would typically interpret your cards. This is a very cool technique that may provide unusual and unexpected insights!

Tarotcise #6: One Word

Super-easy, but so effective! For this Tarotcise, it's all about moving quickly and not overthinking anything.

Shuffle your deck. Don't worry about asking a question. Just pull out a card. Look at it. Say the first word that comes to mind.

Pull another card. Look at it. Say the first word that comes to mind.

Move on to the next card. Repeat. (Continue as long as you'd like!)

Feel free to write down each word—or certain words that feel especially important—if you want to. Later, you can look up each word in a dictionary, a thesaurus, an etymological dictionary (to find the Latin root, Old English root, and/or original meaning of the word), or in a guide to idioms (common sayings and phrases.)

Doing this, do you receive any additional insights?

Maybe one word that came to mind during your Tarotcise was *jealousy*, but then after looking up that word in an etymological dictionary, you discover that the word *jealousy* originally meant "enthusiasm, love, longing, devotion." Aha! Zing! Maybe, with this new information, you have an entirely new perspective on a particular card and how it relates to your life right now.

Tarotcise #7: Two Cards—One Word

This Tarotcise is my favorite method to build speed. Turn over two cards and then choose a word that describes the scenario. Here are a few examples:

- Four of Wands—The Tower = *arson*

- Three of Cups—Two of Cups = *wedding*

- Devil—Nine of Swords = *rehab*

- The Sun—Ace of Wands = *birth*

Try this Tarotcise by yourself or with a friend. It's great fun and sure to get your tarot brain working faster.

Here are some combos to explore:

1. Queen of Wands—Queen of Cups = _____

2. Wheel of Fortune—Ten of Pentacles = _____

3. Strength reversed—Seven of Wands reversed = _____

4. Two of Cups—Three of Cups = _____

5. Three of Pentacles—Ace of Wands = _____

6. Page of Swords—Six of Wands = _____

7. Six of Cups reversed—Five of Cups = _____

8. King of Swords—Ace of Swords = _____

9. Justice—Eight of Swords reversed = _____

10. Knight of Wands—Eight of Wands = _____

Possible answers:

1. *Girlfriends*

2. *Gambling*

3. *Surrender*

4. *Polyamory*

5. *Promotion*

6. *MVP*

7. *Funeral*

8. *Surgeon*

9. *Acquittal*

10. *Adventure*

Do you see how I got those? What about you? What words might you choose instead? Journal your answers.

Tarotcise #8: Guess the Tarot Card

This Tarotcise can be done alone or with one or more friends. Here's how: one person will describe a situation (or the plot of a movie, television show, lyrics, etc.). The other person(s) will guess the tarot cards that most closely fit the situation. Let's look at a few examples:

- In a scene from *Game of Thrones*, Sansa arrives at the Wall and sees Jon Snow after being parted for a long time. The cards: Four of Wands, Ten of Cups, or Six of Cups.

- I'm enrolling in a new online class. The cards: Page of Swords, Ace of Swords.

See how that works? It's like charades . . . for tarot!
Don't have a buddy to work with? Try out these examples:

1. Your boo pops the question.

2. Someone starts an online war.

3. A woman graduates from law school.

4. You are recovering from the flu.

5. A man is in a coma.

6. There is a home invasion.

7. You give birth to twins.

8. You're attending a Jay-Z concert.

9. You get a divorce and begin reentering the dating scene.

10. You're going on a trip to a place you've never been to before.

Here are some possible answers:

1. Ace of Cups, Two of Cups, or Page of Cups. All three have energy around a love offering.

2. Five of Swords, Five of Wands, Ace of Swords. Each of these cards carries an element of conflict.

3. The World, Four of Wands, Six of Wands. These cards show graduation or celebration.

4. Four of Swords, Nine of Swords reversed. Both cards indicate rest and healing.

5. Once again: Four of Swords.

6. Seven of Swords, Five of Swords, the Devil, Tower. This combo shows theft, danger, and upheaval.

7. Empress, Ace of Wands, Two Pages. The Two Pages is key!

8. Four of Wands, Three of Cups. We're having a great time!

9. Three of Swords reversed, Five of Cups reversed, Six of Swords, Ace of Cups. Healing a broken heart and opening up to something new.

10. Eight of Wands, Eight of Cups, the Moon. The Eights show travel; the Moon is a change.

Those are a few examples. Which cards might you pick for those scenarios? Why? Take a minute to journal your answers.

Tarotcise #9: Don't Peek

Shuffle the cards and think of a question. Or you may want to focus on general guidance. Now, pull a card but do *not* turn it over. Sit with the card a few minutes and then journal whatever comes to mind—basically whatever you're feeling from that card without turning it over. No peeking!

Next, leave it alone for the whole day. No matter how curious you are, resist the urge to turn it over.

At the end of your day, sit down with your tarot journal and turn over the card. Which card did you pull? Did it match up with what you wrote? How did the energy show up in your day? Take time to write your notes, including any insights that are coming in.

This is one of my favorite Tarotcises and a great way to start "feeling" the card rather than relying on the image. Play around with it and see what you discover. It's great fun!

Tarotcise #10: Tarot Billets

As I mentioned before, billets are folded slips of paper with questions written on them. The billets are chosen randomly and—without opening them to see the question—you "feel" the answer. It's a great way to work with your intuition.

Here's a tarot spin on it:

Write down a whole bunch of questions on different slips of paper. Fold them up and put them in a hat or jar. Mix them and then randomly pull one out. Hold the note without opening it. No. Peeking. Allowed. Don't read the question inside; just feel the energy.

Grab your tarot cards and shuffle them. Cut the cards. Pull three cards from the top of the deck. Gaze at your cards. Write down your interpretation.

Open your billet and read the question inside. Then look back at the three cards that you pulled out and the interpretation you wrote down. Does your interpretation seem to match the question?

With practice, you might be really surprised by what comes up!

I recommend doing this Tarotcise with a small group of friends—say, around the table at a dinner party. You could each take turns holding the billet, pulling tarot cards, and interpreting. Open the billet after everyone has spoken. This often leads to amazing aha moments! (Or at the very least a very entertaining and memorable dinner party!)

Revisit these warm-ups and Tarotcises often. They will help you become a better, more intuitive tarot reader. So now that you're all nice and stretched, let's put it together.

PART THREE

Road-Testing Your Skills

First Things First

We've gone over tarot card meanings. I've given you lots of Tarotcises and journaling prompts to ponder, as well as solid advice on developing your intuitive muscles. You're ready to road-test this whole tarot shebang! Yeah, baby!

But (you knew there would be a *but*, right?), we must cover a few fundamental pieces so that you can set yourself up for intuitive tarot reading success.

The Best Environment

Years ago, I went to a tarot party on the not-so-great side of town. As I pulled up to the building, I noticed a group of drug dealers on the corner. Bad areas don't really freak me out too much, but it was late, dark, and there was a strange vibe in the air.

I rang the bell, and after a while, a woman came down to greet me. The first thing I noticed was her black eye. She led me up a darkened stairway to a cramped apartment, littered with toys and takeout containers, into the dimly lit kitchen where a few friends had gathered for the party. I don't have good night vision, so my eyes were having trouble adjusting to the room.

I began reading for a man who asked about guns and whether or not his girlfriend was faithful. His eyes darted to the woman with the black eye. Obviously, he was asking about her. Tense as could be, I did my best to deliver helpful, healing readings to the participants—even him.

Suddenly, I caught something moving out of the corner of my eye. As my eyes began to adjust, I saw the walls swarming with roaches and mice crawling around the floor. I gingerly picked up my purse and kept it on my lap for the rest of the party. I couldn't get out of there fast enough.

As I left, I shook my purse out just to make sure I didn't bring any new "friends" home with me. The dealers watched me with a look of both amusement and confusion.

This, my friends, is *not* the type of environment that lends well to a good reading. Look, you can read in any climate (I've read on trains, planes, automobiles, and more), but if you are uncomfortable, your readings will not be as effective. You must create an environment that is calm and supportive.

The right environment is going to look and feel different for everybody. Some people like to be in their home. Others prefer the chatter of a coffee shop. For some, silence is mandatory, whereas others enjoy tinkly spiritual music in the background. What makes you feel safe? What calms your spirit and mind? Consider that.

For myself, I have a quiet office. Gentle music is always playing in the background when I read. A giant mug of hot green tea keeps me hydrated. My chair is a plush purple throne that my cats enjoy using as a bed and scratching post. Around me are books, spiritual art, pictures of my children, and cats. I feel safe here. I don't read at parties or bars, nor do I offer in-person sessions any longer because they don't suit my introvert nature. Plus, I need minimal distractions for my busy Gemini mind.

Your environment may be the same. Or different. Some folks can read under multiple conditions. I suggest testing out reading in different spaces and circumstances. See what works for you and what doesn't. Once you've established your happy place, plant yourself and read your face off.

Keeping It Clean

If you're reading on the regular, you'll want to cleanse your space thoroughly, especially if you're working with a lot of people. Energy sticks. Long after your reading is finished, someone's energetic imprint may still linger in your environment. It needs to be cleansed out to keep the vibe clear.

I cleanse my office every single day. This way, I have an energetically pristine backdrop to do my tarot thing.

Here's what I do.

You'll need:

- Any incense that you like
- A bell
- A selenite wand

Open a window. Light your incense and walk around the room, allowing the smoke to waft into each corner. Silently pray for the vibes to clear. Ask your guides to release any energetic cords from people you've worked with recently.

Next, walk around the perimeter of your reading room with the bell, ringing it in every corner. This breaks up energy.

Finally, take the selenite wand and move it over your body. Selenite is fantastic for cleansing your aura. Sometimes I take crystal quartz and move it around my body in a big clockwise circle and state, "I surround myself with radiant light. Only positive energy can penetrate my aura." This affirmation adds an additional layer of protection so that I can work with people and not take on their energetic stuff.

How to Cleanse Your Tarot Deck

Do you need to cleanse your deck? I think so. Everything is made of energy. Even seventy-eight paper cards. A cleansing of your deck removes psychic debris and keeps your cards running clean. Kind of like an engine.

There are a few ways to do this:

- Light incense and let the smoke waft over your deck. This is an easy way to clear the vibes.

- Create a "crystal sandwich." This is what I do at the end of the workday. You'll need a large crystal and a selenite wand. Put the deck on the crystal. Place the selenite wand on top. Let it rest overnight.

- Put your deck in the window under a new or full moon. This works like a charm.

- A method I love is putting the deck back in order like it's brand-new, starting with the Fool. Then, reshuffle. This method is kind of like rebooting a cell phone. You need to do that every so often for your phone to work well, right? Why not do this with your tarot deck?

In case you're wondering, yes, I cleanse my tarot deck every single day.

Now you're ready to roll, right? Not yet, Grasshopper. There is another vital thing you need to bring to the tarot table: the right mindset. I want to talk about this briefly because if there is one point I'd like to hammer home, it's this: you need to have the right level of openness for intuitive information to flow correctly. Ideally, your querent will also show up with that same mindset. (I'll talk about problem readings soon.) After all, reading is a two-way street. If you're both heading in the same direction, you can get where you want to go faster. Got it? Cool.

Now, remember where I talked about intuition buzzkills in the "Intuition Basics" chapter? I mentioned how skepticism, substances, emotions, and overanalyzing can crush your sixth sense. To recap: don't do that.

I also want to add that expectations and a failure to detach can also hinder your ability to give a good, reliable tarot reading. You'll want to pay attention to both. Let me explain what I mean.

Great Expectations

When you come to a tarot reading as the reader or querent, do you assume that the cards will "see all"? Do you think that every detail will be fleshed out, down to the color of the underwear you're wearing that day? It doesn't work like that. The future isn't some "set-and-forget" agenda where life "just happens to you." It's more complex. That's why a neutral, curious mind on the part of both tarot reader and client is necessary.

If you come with one of these attitudes about tarot, your experience will not be as good:

1. "I'll just wait and see if it will happen." This passive mindset says, "I have no responsibility for how my life will unfold. I'll kick back and wait for things to come true." If you're approaching tarot (or life) with that attitude, you're not being an active participant in your life. For example, a woman came in for a reading and asked if she would meet a man. The cards showed a favorable outcome. A year later she came back and said she didn't meet anyone. When asked what she did to make a connection, she said, "Nothing." She just assumed the reading meant that it would happen without her having to do a thing. Wrong-o. If you are looking for a partner, they usually don't come knocking on your door like one of those lusty plumbers in porn movies. Life requires you to make an effort. A reading shows potential, but that doesn't mean you get to lounge on the couch in your PJs and wait around eating bonbons.

2. "I hope it happens . . . ," usually accompanied by a long sigh. This bummer mind-set means you are only expecting the negative. If that's you, you'll find a way to sabotage your life, no matter how good the cards might be.

3. "That can't happen." Those who have this mindset are closed to any information that may come through. It doesn't matter how accurate the information is because their mind is already made up, and even if something rings true, they'll assume that trickery was involved.

It's crucial for both people sitting at the tarot table to remain open and curious. When the reading is approached in that manner, the chances for it being helpful are amplified.

Detachment

The other side of the tarot mindset coin is detachment—the ability to remain objective. In other words, you must be able to get your feelings and experiences out of the way, so nothing colors the information.

For example, if you have strong feelings about a question or situation, that may create bias. Same with wanting a particular outcome. While there is nothing wrong with wanting to see a positive future, if you are too invested in that, you may see only what you want to see instead of what's actually coming through.

Detachment doesn't mean being a cold fish or Mr. Spock, however. You can still have all the feels, but you must be mindful that they are not infecting the reading; otherwise, you risk projection, which puts your experiences and opinions into the mix.

How do you do that?

For one, you must be aware of your triggers. If you feel yourself bristling at a question or situation, that's a sign that you may be biased. Let me give an example: I despise gambling. In my opinion, it's a waste of money, and any questions about winning money give me agita. The only time I've been in a casino was once for an art show. I was so uncomfortable looking at the people at the slot machines that I had to get the hell out of there!

Because I know this about myself, I also am aware that I do not like reading about gambling. I won't give numbers or anything like that. Years ago, a man asked me about his casino habit. The cards were negative. The next time I saw him, he griped that I had "ruined his luck" and that the tarot "put him on a losing streak." I'm not sure if it was the accuracy of the cards or my lousy attitude giving him trouble, but I knew then that this wasn't my forte.

Once you know what sets you off, let querents know immediately if they ask a question you don't like. This way, you keep it honest and remove yourself from giving a loaded reading.

Another thing I recommend is letting people know when you're stating your opinion or experience versus what's in the cards. For example, if someone inquires about a situation that I have a particular judgement toward, I will put the cards to the side and say, "Before we look at the cards around this situation, I want to give you my opinion, so we don't mix the two up." This straightforward approach keeps the reading clean because now I've stated what I feel right off the bat.

Same with life experience. Always let the other person know up front if you have had a similar situation . . . and then get on with the cards. For example, let's say someone inquires about a nasty divorce. Maybe you went through the same thing. Saying "I've been where you have; let's see what the cards have to say about your situation" lets the client know that you understand what is happening, but you're going to the cards for wisdom.

When you share your experiences or opinions, be candid but brief. I find that stating this out loud serves to keep the air clear and the reader grounded in the moment and focused on the client instead of getting mired in their own stuff.

Now that we have that out of the way, let's read tarot!

How to Shuffle

How you shuffle depends on what feels natural to you. As I like to say: shuffle as if you were about to play a game of poker. Don't overthink it. Just shuffle the damn cards.

Some folks are gentle and timid, and others prefer making fancy-pants bridges. Other people enjoy spreading the cards facedown on the table and swirling them around like an enormous mandala. It's really up to you.

If you allow others to shuffle your deck, keep in mind that you may go through a lot more decks. Years ago, I had a woman shuffle a brand-new deck so aggressively that she destroyed it in one sitting. (Interesting: she was a rather aggressive, angry sort of person too.) Be sure to purchase decks printed on sturdy card stock, and keep a few extras on hand should you decide to let other people handle them.

How will you know how long to shuffle? Shuffle as long as you feel comfortable . . . or until you get bored. That simple.

Next, put the deck facedown on the table. Using your left hand, cut the deck into three piles. Then put them back together any way you wish.

Why the left hand? The left is closer to your heart, which means the reading comes from your heart. Frankly, this is a superstition, and I'm left-handed, so I like it, but you don't need to use this cutting method if you're not called to . . . or if you're not a southpaw.

Tarotcise

Before reading the cards, take a peek at the bottom of the deck. That card will give a clue! For example, let's say you're doing a general outlook for a woman. You turn over the Six of Cups; that means she's most likely thinking about family or past love. Now, lay out the cards and start reading. How does that bottom card influence the reading . . . or not?

How to Ask Good Questions

A good tarot reading begins with a good question. That being said, general outlooks, which we will cover soon, can be helpful. Even so, I prefer that I have an area to focus on; this way, I don't waste my time or the client's time.

For example, when I work with another reader, I'm always up front. I want to know about business and money. I don't care about romance (my love life is solid), and I am superstitious about health, so I don't want to hear about it. That's pretty blunt, right? Perhaps. But I find that being straight-up leads to a reading that is useful rather than have the reader guess what I need to know. A "cold call" type of reading with zero background information can be impressive, especially when the reader pulls out things I can validate. But for some reason, when I receive those types of readings, I end up getting useless information about my love life and less about the things I care about. (Not sure why so many readers assume I have some sort of scandalous romance going on—I don't.)

I recommend that you have clear questions before you approach the tarot table. You'll also want to encourage anyone who sits with you to come prepared as well.

Structure the questions, so they are helpful. "Will I" is one of the least useful inquiries. It creates a passive approach to life. Like I said before, life doesn't just happen to you. The cards can show the possibilities, but you still have to do your part.

Another question that isn't constructive is "Should I." This question puts your decisions in someone else's hands. That's not taking responsibility for your life. It's removing your role and making someone else responsible for how things turn out. You'll want to avoid that and encourage your querent to reframe those questions.

"Yes/No" questions are a mixed bag. In some cases, they can be helpful, but that assumes there is no choice in the matter. While some situations are cut and dried, many are not.

I like formatting questions like this:

What do I need to know about _____?

What can I expect if I do _____?

What might be the results if I make this decision_____?

How can I _____?

When you format your questions like that, you can look at possible outcomes, but also you can glean advice, which makes the future much more empowering.

Let's look at a few questions revamped:

Will I marry Sebastian?

What do I need to know about my relationship with Sebastian?

Should I quit my job?

What can I expect if I quit my job?

Will I go back to school?

What might be the results if I go back to school?

Will I meet a new woman?

How can I meet a new partner?

Once again, the reframed questions make a world of difference.

Some readers don't think it's right to reframe questions for the querent. In some cases, I don't, even if I don't think the question asked will lead to helpful information. Instead, I'll quietly ask my guides for illumination so that even if I'm getting a poorly worded question, I can still look for the useful nuggets that will empower my client.

Other Things to Be Mindful of When Asking Questions

Some questions cross ethical lines. For example, some things are none of your business. Asking about your ex's new relationship? Not your business. Want to know if your boss is into kinky sex? Nope. Wondering about someone's sexual orientation? This isn't of any concern to you.

Prying into the affairs of people who are not present at the time of the reading is a no-no. Of course, there are exceptions. A mother wanting to know how to help her child who is struggling with addiction? Yes. If you're coming from the angle of wanting to know if someone is okay or how you could help that person, that's fine. Just be careful that whatever you're asking isn't meddling into situations that are not your business.

Also, you'll want to avoid questions about health and legal matters. Unless you are a licensed therapist, doctor, or lawyer, you should not give advice in these areas. If someone asks, you might want to look at the energy around the situation but refer them to the proper professionals. If you take on a client's medical questions and try to diagnose or prescribe, you risk getting sued. So, it's not just an ethical issue; it's also a liability.

That being said, people will often inquire about these situations. I always preface by saying "I'm not a doctor/lawyer/therapist, so therefore I cannot diagnose/prescribe/give legal advice/offer therapy. All I can do is look at the energy around the situation. You'll need to discuss your situation with the proper person, so I will advise you to seek counsel with a health-care practitioner/therapist/attorney that you trust."

Another situation that walks a fine ethical line is talking about death. I've had countless people ask, "When am I going to die?" Usually, this is someone who is trying to play games, but on occasion, some folks are serious. I do not recommend entertaining this query. First, you don't want to frighten anyone. Second, this sort of information could be dangerous in the wrong hands.

There are exceptions to every rule, however. For example, I had a terminally ill client come to my office with her granddaughter in tow. This client had a few weeks to live and wanted to know how everyone would fare after she was gone. My job was to make sure she felt ready for what was ahead and comforted in the knowledge that her loved ones would go on just fine. In this case, she was asking about the impact on her family from her impending death. I broke the rules because it was appropriate to the situation, and it turned out to be one of the most meaningful readings I have ever done.

Sometimes people will be deliberately vague when asking questions because they have an agenda. The agenda could be to "test you," or something else may be going on and they don't want to divulge. In those situations, you'll want to pry a little just in case.

Let me give you another example. A client came to me and wanted to know if his "plan would work out." The cards showed that the plan would indeed work out perfectly. For some reason, I felt "off" about this response, so I asked him what his plan was. He said he was going to kill himself. I put the cards aside, and we had a long talk about getting help. When he left the office, I once again broke another rule: I called his loved ones and expressed my concerns. Client confidentiality is a must for a tarot reader, but in this case, I was not going to sit back and do nothing and have that on my conscience. Needless to say, the family got him help, and he is thriving today.

Tarotcise

Practice rewording questions using the format shown here. Write down a bunch of random queries such as "Will John call me tonight?" and "Should I quit my job?" and read from that perspective. Then change them around to my suggested formats and see how that approach works.

Start to Read

When you're doing a tarot reading, the images speak for themselves. Laying out the cards, you begin to see a story emerge. In a way, the spread is like a little storyboard that shows what's happening.

Look how the cards go together. Do the images face each other? How do they interact . . . or not? Are there are a lot of reversals? Mostly Majors? Minors? What's missing?

Scan the spread. Notice what catches your eye. Examine each card. Look closely. What colors or figures seem to stand out? Is there one card that calls to you? Another one that doesn't make sense?

In a way, you're like a true detective, searching for clues and trying to determine what's happening and how that may play out in the future.

Ask questions. What does the querent have to say about a particular card? Are they reacting to any cards or not? How does that make you feel? Look at every card thoroughly and how they connect as closely as possible. Then begin interpretation.

Interpretation

Interpretation isn't just reading the cards based on the standard tarot card meaning. Those meanings serve a role, but you do not want to get hung up on them. They are simply a touchstone. Your intuition does the work piecing everything together in a cohesive story.

Here's an example. Let's say you are asking about your job. Things have been dicey lately, and you're not sure if you want to stay or go. The cards you pull:

- Death, Five of Swords, and Four of Pentacles reversed

Now, if you look at the traditional meanings, you see change (Death), dishonesty (Five of Swords), and let go (Four of Pentacles reversed). That's clear as a bell, right? But what if your intuition sees something different here? Perhaps the interpretation might be leaning in another direction. It might be saying: "A major change has been happening behind the scenes. It's almost like someone else is coming in and making waves. This feels like a hostile takeover. The person in charge is about to lose their crown. Someone is taking their power away from them."

This was an actual reading I did for someone. Instead of telling the client to let go and move on, I saw a need to be prepared. That person loved their job, and they sat tight while a hostile takeover raged on for months. The manager was fired, and the new person cleaned up a toxic environment, which should have happened long ago. My client was fine and still works there to this day.

Another example: one of my friends was reading for someone, and I don't remember much about it except the Eight of Cups at the end. He said, "You're going away." The other person asked if it was for a trip. He said, "Nope. Looks more like jail or prison." The querent seemed perplexed and walked away. Sure enough, years later, that person got busted and went away for a few years. When I read about it in the news, all I could think of was that Eight of Cups.

This is how intuitive reading works. The Eight of Cups is traditionally seen as "moving on, travel, or seeking." But the reader saw something different and went with his gut.

How do you know when to go with the traditional meaning and when to use your instincts? I always obey the instinct first. Even if the interpretation seems off the wall, don't ignore it. It might turn out to be important later.

When you are first starting out, you might be a bit timid with your interpretations. That's okay. Go slow. Use the meanings in this book or the little white book that came with your deck. As you begin to find your intuitive muscles, you will rely on those interpretations less and less. Soon, you'll ditch them, like a child speeding off on a new bike, the training wheels lying by the side of the road.

How do you know when that day will come? You're barely glancing at the book. Instead, you're going with your gut and letting the images tell the story. I knew I was ready when the information began to spill out of me like a ticker tape. Suddenly, my words were coming so fast that there was no time to check what the cards "meant." My sixth sense took over, and I've never looked back.

Today, my readings still are pretty much like that. I lay out the cards, and the information comes automatically like I'm a rapper in a rap battle! In fact, I hate when a client interrupts because it ruins my flow! In time, you may be the same. That comes with practice.

The Prediction Predicament

What about the future? Can we reliably see what's coming? Well, yes and no. We can see where actions may be leading, but there is always the possibility that you will misinterpret information or the querent may decide to make a change.

There are also times when we're so focused on one aspect of our lives that other important issues may be overlooked. When that happens, we wonder, "How come we didn't see that in the cards?"

One of my clients had a brother who was involved in a gang. Over the years, he managed to stay out of trouble, but he never entirely left those roots. It's not easy to walk from that life. My client came in for a reading, and we talked about the usual: romance, kids, money. A few months later, she called me to say that her brother had been murdered. She was upset that the cards "didn't see" this. How could they miss something so important? "You never asked about him," I replied.

Keep in mind that our guides (or other people) may throw a monkey wrench into a reading. Perhaps on some level, you don't want to know the answer. Or maybe your higher guidance does not wish for your interference. Maybe karma has a say in how events will unfold. Also, while I believe we can see "likely outcomes," our choices, as well as the decisions made by other people, can change everything. Karma, free will, and other folks all play a part in what the future may hold. As readers, we do our best but must understand that no one can "see it all."

As Run-DMC says: "It's tricky."

This may be why many readers shy away from divination. It's not easy and requires lots of practice. Even then, life can throw a few furious curveballs.

Recently, a long-term client had a session scheduled with me. I waited around, and she didn't call on time, which was unusual. I sent her an email and tried to call. Nothing. This had me a bit worried, because in the thirty years we have worked together, this has never happened. An hour later, she called and apologized. It turns out she was traveling and got the time zones mixed up. She rescheduled for a few weeks down the road.

When this client and I reconnected, there were dramatic changes in her life. Her father had passed unexpectedly. He recently traveled to spend the week with her family. They went out for dinner, and when they returned home, he fell. He was rushed to the hospital, and the doctor suggested surgery. But he refused. He said he was happy with his dinner and content because he was with his favorite daughter.

He passed away peacefully a few hours later at her home. As we discussed this, we both wondered if there was divine intervention on his behalf. Were his guides aware that he was "ready to go" and made sure that she was not on the horn with me, getting a possible warning? Perhaps they knew that I might see that he was ill. Or maybe not. We'll never know. But one thing we both agreed on: there was some sort of intervention, because in all the time we have worked together, this sort of botched appointment has never happened.

Some tarot readers are anti-prediction. They rail against it and try to make any reader who enjoys divination feel bad. If they had their way, there would be no more predictive tarot readers.

I find that way of thinking odd because when people come to a tarot reading, even if you claim that predictions are not part of your bag of tricks, it's what most folks want. They come to know what may be ahead, how their decisions might pan out, and what to avoid. They want to know what's in the cards. Even readers who say that they don't do divination ultimately end up doing some form of it.

If you feel that you don't want to attempt prediction, that is totally up to you. After all, it's not easy. You can be wrong. And it sucks balls when you are. Feel free to leave that to the folks who enjoy taking the risk.

By that same token, don't disrespect people who enjoy it. Tarot can be used however people feel called. There is no "one way." Modern readers use tarot for life coaching, therapy, creative inspiration, introspection, and more. It's all good. Find what works for you and go for it. And let everyone else do the same.

As far as readings that attempt to see the future, there is nothing unethical about them. Sometimes it helps to have an idea of what's up ahead. That allows you to make brave decisions.

Like I said before, I like to say that predictive tarot is like driving a car. You're zipping down the road, and suddenly another car is coming in your direction with lights blinking at you. If you've driven a car, you know what that means: there is a speed trap ahead. Now you have a choice. You can continue driving over the limit, and the most likely outcome will be a speeding ticket. Or you can slow down . . . and change your future.

This is how I approach the predictive process.

Tarotcise

 First thing in the morning, pull a tarot card. Without taking time to analyze the card, write down your prediction for the day. Use this format: "Today I will _____." At the end of the day, check in and see: did your prediction come true? For example, if you pull the Page of Pentacles reversed, you might say, "Today I will get bad news about money." Let's say you get a larger than expected credit card bill. Yay! You called it. But what if you don't? What if the day goes by with no news about your cash flow? Look back and see if there might be any other way to interpret the card. If you still feel flummoxed, put it aside and revisit it in a few days.

Journaling prompt: What do you think about divination? Do you think the future is set in stone?

The Fastest Way to Grow Your Skills

Daily practice will build your skills, but if you want to get up to speed, the best way is to read for as many other people as you can. Read for every demographic and situation. Bring out the cards in public places. Read for people solo, read for groups. Sign up to do a tarot party for free and read all night long. Consider it your boot camp or initiation.

The more you read and more people you read, the better you'll get.

In the beginning, you may be shy, but take a deep breath and read anyway. You're gonna be wrong at times. That's okay. Keep going.

The Spreads

In this book, we only concern ourselves with three spreads:

- One-card draws

- Past Present Future

- The Celtic Cross

Why?

In my opinion, these three are the best for intuitive readings as well as general outlooks. A general outlook is a reading done with little to no backstory from the client. The querent may want to know about the future or just get some general guidance. This type of reading requires a great deal of skill, practice, and confidence with your intuition. But don't sweat this! I'm going to walk you through each spread with sample readings.

For each reading, we'll do two different samples. The first one will be a specific question, and the second will be a general outlook.

One-Card Draws

Someone (I can't remember who) once said to me that one card contains all the information that you need. This person also said that you should be able to deliver a ton of guidance with just that one card. While that may seem like a mighty tall order (or challenge), there is some truth to this advice. Each card is rich in symbolism, and you can find plenty to work with for interpreting.

Let's start by using the one-card draw for a question. Sabine's daughter just got married. She's already talking about starting a family. Naturally, Sabine is excited at the prospect of becoming a first-time grandmother. Her question: "What can I expect when it comes to anticipating future grandchildren?" (I have to laugh at her clever way of avoiding a "will I" question.)

The card she pulled: Eight of Swords. The woman in the card is certainly not moving. She's wearing a blindfold and is bound. Sabine said, "I guess this means it's out of my control." I agreed. I also noted that the answer is not here at this time, and the question about children might be more effective if her daughter were asking instead. Also, perhaps it is too soon to visit this question since her daughter *just* got married. Sabine will need to wait this out and not put pressure on her daughter. While this card may not seem like a positive one to see, it is tarot's way of reminding Sabine to remain focused on her own world rather than getting too nosy about her daughter's.

Now, let's do a general outlook, no question. Sabine chose the Three of Wands. This card shows a bright future and many possibilities on the horizon. My interpretation: "You're at the top of your game at this time. You've worked hard to get there. If you look at the present moment, you'll see that you are standing on a mountain of accomplishments. You'll also see that ships are sailing into view, a sign that new opportunities are on the way. Soon, you'll have a few good options to consider. Where do you want to go from here? What do you want to conquer next? Set your sights on your big, bold future, and know that everything is possible. If you're thinking about travel, this card promises more than one journey ahead."

Sabine is currently at the peak of her career. She's in her mid-fifties and holds a high position in a corporate job. Travel is something on the docket for the next year, and much of it revolves around major career deals.

How did I get that? I just trusted my gut and let the card do the talking. Keep in mind that this is my interpretation. You may see other things for Sabine.

Tarotcise

Pull out the cards mentioned in these examples. What information might you give Sabine in either case? What are you seeing that I'm not? Journal your thoughts.

After-Dinner Tarot Mints

One night after a lovely dinner in a Moroccan restaurant in the East Village, my friend Paige Zaferiou pulled out the tiniest tarot deck I have ever seen for some impromptu readings. This was great fun, and I said it was like an "after-dinner tarot mint."

Since that time, I've always had a baby tarot deck with me for dinner-tainment and on-the-go tarot readings. I've been known to pull out the deck randomly while standing in line at the coffee shop or meeting strangers at a bar. Reading the cards spontaneously is a fantastic way to sharpen your skills and make connections. After all, everyone loves having their cards read!

At one such dinner, I began experimenting with a technique that is great fun . . . and revelatory. It's a way to add an extra element of oomph to a one-card spread; plus it brings people together. I call it my Round Robin Tarot Reading.

Here's how you do it:

You need four people. Any more than that, and the reading becomes unwieldy. Three can work, but two people aren't enough. I've found through experimentation that four is the ideal number.

One person shuffles the cards and then fans them out, facedown. Each person at the table draws one card. That person can choose a specific question or general advice. Once everyone has pulled a card, each person takes a turn, interpreting what they think their card means. The other people at the table can offer their interpretation too.

Next, one at a time, all the participants use all four cards to do a reading for themselves, starting with their card and going around the table to the left in the order they are sitting. For example, let's say I'm sitting at the table with Paige to my left, followed by Briana and Hilary. I'll start with my card, then read Paige's, and next Briana's, and finally Hilary's. This will be my reading with Hilary's card as my outcome.

Paige will then do her reading starting with her card, followed by Briana's, Hilary's, and mine will be last. And so on. What's interesting about the Round Robin Tarot Reading is that we all have unique interpretations, but once we add the other participants' cards with our own, the readings are uncanny.

After everyone is finished, I lay out the cards, and we do a reading for the world with the four cards chosen.

This technique is a playful twist on a one-card draw and a perfect way to end a night out with your besties!

Past Present Future

The Past Present Future spread is an oldie but a goodie. Every tarot book on the market has this spread or some version of it. It's excellent for divination purposes and specific questions.

The way to do the spread: Shuffle the cards, focusing on the question or just keeping your mind open. Cut the cards into three piles and put them back together. Take three cards off the top of the deck and turn them over. The positions are Past, Present, and Future. You can look at them as a whole and interpret that way or use the positions.

Let's look at some examples. Xavier wants to see where his new relationship with Paul is heading. The cards he pulls: Nine of Wands, Five of Swords reversed, Queen of Cups.

Past: Nine of Wands—Xavier has been hurt before. He's coming into this relationship with a lot of baggage. The old scars have never been fully healed. He may even have unfinished business with an ex! His trust issues are massive, so his new relationship is going to have a rough start.

Present: Five of Swords reversed—I always interpret the Five of Swords as a card of hurt and deception. Reversed, it seems to say that the new partner is proving that he can be trusted. Paul is being honest and wants to keep the air as clean as possible. Perhaps he's aware that Xavier has trust issues and is being delicate. Or maybe he's looking to move forward and doesn't want Xavier's past to get in the way of a promising future.

Future: Queen of Cups—Speaking of the future, the Queen of Cups is a sweet card to see in a love reading. There is a possibility for a real, genuine heart connection here. Even if Xavier has reservations, Paul may be able to break through those old wounds and help Xavier learn to trust in love again. My feeling is that this relationship may have some challenges, but if they continue to work on building trust, it could become a profound, loving union.

Now, let's do a general outlook for Xavier.

The cards: Strength, Eight of Cups, Ace of Cups.

  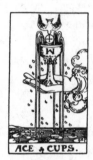

Past: Strength—Xavier has overcome a significant challenge. Something in his life felt difficult. It required him to rely on his inner strength more than ever before. In some way, this situation has forced him to deal with unpleasantness, but perhaps it made him stronger. The challenge is well behind him, and he's come out on top.

Present: Eight of Cups—He's moved on. The past is in the past. There are still some unresolved emotions, but he's left the challenge in search of something new. When I look at these two cards, I see a person who got sick of struggling and decided to walk away.

Future: Ace of Cups—A new beginning, new love, and the new emotional beginning are on the way. Xavier left a situation that was not working, and now he's about to embark on a new emotional journey, one that will be healing. New love is offered. Even if he thought he would be alone, this combination tells me that he won't. He has much to look forward to.

If we looked at these cards without relying on the positions, we might notice the two cards from the Cups suit and determine that a lot is happening in the client's sentimental life. The energy between these three cards shows a person on a journey to love or in the midst of an emotional rebirth.

Your turn!

Tarotcise

Pull out the cards that Xavier chose for each spread and contemplate your interpretations for the cards. How do they go together? What are the general themes? If you had to tell a story for each spread, what might the story be? Journal your thoughts and any advice you'd give Xavier.

Bonus Tarotcise

Now, using the same cards, let the first spread be a general outlook, and use the cards in the second spread for the question. What interpretations might you find when you change things around? Are things different? What themes are present in both readings? Does the future look different if you move the cards around?

In the second reading, read the cards from right to left as if you are telling the story backward. What does this tell you? How does the story look when you go back?

The Celtic Cross

The Celtic Cross is one of the most popular tarot spreads. This ten-card layout packs a lot of punch and allows for a rich, detailed tarot reading. It can be used to get in-depth answers to a question. It's also useful for general outlooks because the positions create a trail of clues that can show where a querent has been and where they may be heading.

The Celtic Cross layout involves six cards in a cross formation and a vertical row of four on the right side of the cross (see the image on page 222).

There are variations on how the cards should be laid out—often with positions 3 and 5 reversed. In my opinion, the way that makes the most sense is to place position 3 on the bottom and lay 4, 5, and 6 clockwise around the mini-cross in the middle.

Here's how to lay out the Celtic Cross and a brief description of what each position means:

- 1—This is the present moment; where you are right now; the heart of the matter; where things stand.

- 2—This is what crosses you, for good or ill. Position 2 shows potential obstacles or support. Put this card over position 1 to form a small cross.

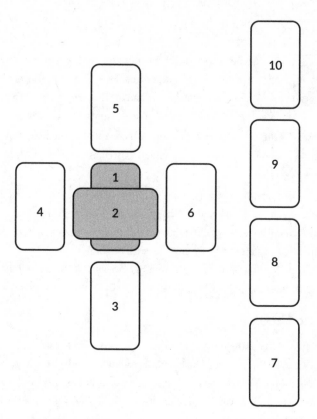

- 3—This is the foundation of the situation or the past conditions that have led to the present. It's where you're coming from. The source. This card is placed below the mini-cross.

- 4—This is the recent past or the things that are just starting to move into the background. The energy of this card may still be lingering, but it's on the way out. This card sits to the left of the mini-cross.

- 5—Situations on the horizon or what may come into being, the possibilities. Some people say, "This is what crowns you." It may reflect where you want to go. This card goes above the mini-cross.

TAROT: NO QUESTIONS ASKED

- 6—This is the near future or what is coming or developing from the situation. Place this card to the right of the mini-cross.

- 7—This is the querent at the moment. This can reflect the querent's current position . . . or the prevailing attitude toward the situation. This card is the bottom of the vertical column to the right of the cross.

- 8—This is the environment, surroundings, or other influences. This position can be the home or work environment, as well as other people who may be influencing the situation. Place this card above position 7.

- 9—This is the hopes and fears of the querent. It can also symbolize the shadow work needing to be done. Position 9 is above 8.

- 10—This is the outcome or where you're headed. Once you interpret this card, you might choose additional spreads to decide on courses of action, especially if the outlook seems unfavorable. The last card will be placed above 9.

When you lay out the cards in this formation, you'll see that position 3 as the foundation makes sense. As you move clockwise around the mini-cross, a story unfolds from the past influences toward the likely outcome. It's fluid and reads well.

Some readers will pick a significator to represent the querent before they shuffle the cards. This is a matter of personal preference. I don't do this because I believe that the energy the person is manifesting at the time of the reading will show up in the reading. (More on significators in the "Fine-Tuning Your Intuitive Tarot Readings" chapter.)

Methodology

You've laid out the Celtic Cross. Now what?

The Initial Scan

Begin by scanning the cards. Without examining the cards too deeply, what is your initial impression? Which cards are getting your attention? Are there any that don't seem to be "speaking" to you?

Next, look for the overarching theme. What are the majorities? Which suits are missing? For example, let's say that the cards are mostly Majors. This tells you right off the bat that big lessons are happening at this time, and a certain amount of fate may be involved.

Mostly Minors? It's all day-to-day grind and an indicator that things are within our control. Fate has little to say or do with the situation, or actions or lack thereof are creating the conditions.

A full set of Court cards? Lots of people involved.

See how that works?

Take stock of what's standing out, and you'll have a foundation to begin your reading. Here are a few more examples of multiples and what they could be telling you:

- All Minors—this shows a focus on the normal affairs of daily life.

- All Majors (this is *rare*)—heavy karmic period.

- Mostly Swords—significant conflicts.

- Mostly Pentacles—focus on money, material side of life.

- Mostly Cups—lots of emotion; attention on relationships.

- Mostly Wands—career focus.

- Mostly high numbers—you're nearing the completion of a situation.

- Mostly low numbers—you're at the very beginning of a situation.

- Lots of Aces—I always see this as a good thing—fresh starts and opportunities!

- Lots of Twos—big decision-making time.

- Lots of Threes—birth, creativity, positive change.

- Lots of Fours—excellent stability.

- Lots of Fives—significant changes, difficulties.

- Lots of Sixes—overall harmony.

- Lots of Sevens—many challenges to be overcome.

- Lots of Eights—success!

- Lots of Nines—endings are inevitable.

- Lots of Tens—closure and new chapters.

- Mostly reversals—mostly reversals symbolize an internal process or lots of delays and blockages.

Also note if there are multiple Court members:

- Three or more Pages—day care, school, many new beginnings.

- Three or more Knights—college, a time of great action.

- Three or more Queens—feminine leadership, gossip.

- Three of more Kings—important meetings, government.

Sweep your eyes over the cards, take note of what cards are making up the lion's share of the reading, and start breaking down the spread into manageable sections.

The first section to consider is the mini-cross in the middle. This will give you the lowdown of how things stand at the moment. Are the cards in harmony? Do they support each other, or is there a contradiction present? For example, are they both positive in nature, or is one negative? What might two gloomy-looking cards tell you about the situation? How about two happy ones? What if the first card is negative and the crossing card is positive? Or vice versa?

Next, Examine the Other Card Pairings

Positions 3 and 4 give you an idea of what has created this moment in time. What can you glean about the past from those two cards?

If you compare positions 4 and 6, you see what's just leaving and what's on the way. For example, if you pulled the Six of Pentacles for position 4 and Five of Pentacles for 6, you'd see a financial setback, such as losing your source of support.

Pair positions 7 and 9, and you get a glimpse of how the querent is thinking about their situation. But if you take 7 and 8, you see how the environment might be supporting the person . . . or not. This pair could be important because your environment, including the people in it, can influence how things might unfold.

Look at positions 5 and 10 to get an idea of where it's all heading. For example, let's say you have the Knight of Cups in position 5 and the Emperor in 10. This could indicate a marriage proposal is on the way.

After you've moved through those pairings, begin breaking down the spread into groups. This helps construct the cohesive story the cards are trying to tell. I look at groups of three and four.

Here Are the Threes

Past (3), Recent Past (4), Present (1)—Once again, we can see how the story developed.

Present (1), Obstacle (2), Querent (7)—This combo is the present moment and how the querent is standing (or not).

Querent (7), Environment (8), Hopes and Fears (9)—These three cards give a clear idea of not only the mindset but also the things that might be influencing thoughts or actions.

Possible Future (5), Near Future (6), Likely Outcome (10)—These three cards neatly sum up the likely future.

The Past (3), Near Future (6), Likely Outcome (10)—This diagonal mini-spread shows the root, what's next, and potential. It's like a Past Present Future contained within the spread. If you're in a pinch, these are the three go-to cards for a fast 'n furious interpretation.

Here Are the Fours

Past (3), Present (1), Obstacle (2), Possible Future (6)—Here, we see the potential based on the past.

Recent Past (4), Present (1), Obstacle (2), Near Future (6)—These four give a snapshot of the most recent and soon-to-be events.

Querent (7), Environment (8), Hopes and Fears (9), Likely Outcome (10)—The column gives you an idea of everything that might be influencing the future. Is there something that needs to be changed?

I can size up a reading quickly by taking a minute to skim over the images and see what's standing out. It may seem like a lot to digest when you first begin. But with time and practice, the scan becomes second nature.

Tarotcise

Lay out a Celtic Cross. Take out your journal. Begin counting up the majorities. What's standing out? Now, pair up the cards. How do the pairings work together? Is there a conflict? Write down your answers in your journal. Now do a few more Celtic Crosses and try to build speed.

Tarotcise

Use the Celtic Cross for a particular question. Do a series of mini-readings only using the Threes. Write down your answers to each of these small readings in your journal.

Major Karma

If your Celtic Cross has four or more Majors, it's a sign that you may be working through a critical karmic lesson. In other words: transformation is happening on some level.

I've created a little formula based on one of Eileen Connolly's books, *Tarot: The First Handbook for the Master*. Her approach is different from mine and involves a lot more shuffling. I prefer a speedier way, so I stick to the cards that are already present in the reading.

Here's what to do:

After you've completed the initial reading, pull the four (or more) Majors out of the spread and line them up in order from the first Major pulled to the last one.

This forms an additional spread. The positions are as follows:

- Card 1: The Lesson

- Card 2: The Current Position on the Karmic Path

- Card 3: The Direction Ahead on the Karmic Path

- Card 4 (and any additional cards): Reflection

Let's use an example. Piper inquired about her relationship with Robert. After many years together, the spark was gone. Yet they couldn't seem to "quit each other," she said. The higher number of Major Arcana cards in her reading showed that there might be a spiritual lesson to the situation.

The cards were Judgement, Death reversed, Strength, Tower reversed, Empress.

Here are the interpretations:

- Card 1: The Lesson—Judgement. Judgement signals a wake-up call, rebirth, or awakening. Piper seems to be getting a text memo from the Universe that something is coming to an end. A situation requires closure. Is it the relationship? Or is there a need to forgive a transgression? Whatever the case may be, Judgement says: let this go, start fresh, and seek the higher ground.

- Card 2: The Current Position on the Karmic Path—Death reversed. Limbo. There is no movement at all. While the Judgement card cries out for a transformation, this reversal says: something needs to give. Someone is resisting change. Could it be that both Piper and Robert are in denial, unwilling to face the painful truth that the relationship is on life support, barely breathing?

- Card 3: The Direction Ahead on the Karmic Path—Strength. Courage will be needed to overcome the situation. This card shows a challenge being handled through willpower. They may slowly wake up from their slumber and realize what they have. This moment will give them the will to face the issues, and with love, they may be able to heal the problems that got them into this situation.

- Card 4 (and any additional cards): Reflection—Tower reversed, Empress. The Tower reversed indicates that they may want to reflect on what they stand to lose if they do not fix the foundation of their relationship. It's also a sign that perhaps they are holding on because, on some level, they know this is worth fixing and the problems are not so significant that they cannot be resolved. The Empress is a reminder that there is love and commitment. If they focus on rebuilding, the relationship can flourish.

In short: the resistance is karmic in nature, because on some deeper level, they both know that this relationship isn't finished. With work and love, they can emerge a stronger, more loving couple.

Tarotcise

Consider the plotline for a movie. Pull out four Majors from your deck. Using the positions above, determine what the karmic lesson might be for the characters in the film.

Where to Start from Here?

After you examine the cards and patterns, it's time to start laying down your interpretation! Let those words flow like a rap song. Do not stop to think about what you're saying too much. Allow the images to speak to you and through you. Share the story that is unfolding without filtering your answers. Let the information pour out of your mouth like a ticker tape. This is how I read, and like I said before, it's why I get salty when folks interrupt me. It disrupts my rhythm.

You might say: "Well, that's all well and good, Theresa. But you've been at this for a while. Where on earth do I start?" You can start anywhere you feel called. What card is grabbing your attention? Begin from that point and circle around as your intuition guides you.

But if you're stuck and not sure what to do first, always begin with the card at the very bottom of the spread (3). After all, this is the root and perfect jumping-off point for following the story the reading is trying to tell. From there, move to position 4, the recent past followed by the mini-cross. This is the starting route I usually follow.

From there, wind your way around the layout from 5 to 10. Once you've gone through every card, take a moment to see if there are any additional insights. Maybe you notice that the majority of the cards have a yellow background. What does that add to the reading? Or perhaps you get a feeling to go back to the mini-cross for some reason. If so, why? Remain curious and open. If you're reading for someone else, ask the querent if any cards are grabbing their attention. Explore that. Allow them to add their thoughts to what each card may mean. Create a conversation, and you may uncover new, helpful information.

The tarot cards will help you see the story. You just need to trust that your intuition guide the narration.

Sample Readings

We're going to use the Celtic Cross two ways. First, we'll do a reading based on a specific question. Then, we'll do a general outlook.

Reading One: Specific Question

The first reading is for my client Moriah, who runs her own creative enterprise. Things have slowed down in the past few months, and she's concerned about her finances and the state of her business. Here are the cards she pulled:

- 1—Seven of Pentacles

- 2—Knight of Wands

- 3—Eight of Cups

- 4—The Hierophant

- 5—Eight of Wands

- 6—Six of Pentacles

- 7—Ten of Pentacles

- 8—Strength

- 9—Three of Cups

- 10—King of Swords

As I scan the reading, I notice the three cards from the Pentacles suit—Seven of Pentacles, Six of Pentacles, Ten of Pentacles. Because this is a question about money and business, that's the first thing I look for.

Reading One

Next, I check to see if there is anything particularly detrimental in the reading. Nope. I see a few challenges here with the Strength card and Seven of Pentacles, but overall, the cards are neutral or positive.

The next thing I see is mostly high numbers. Two Eights, a Six, a Seven, and a Ten. That tells me that she's at the tail end of a situation. Even if she is experiencing a bad run at this time, there is an end in sight.

What catches my eye next are the cards symbolizing the future: Eight of Wands, Six of Pentacles, and King of Swords. This combination seems to indicate an improvement ahead. We are not heading into troubled waters. Instead, there is a light at the end of the tunnel.

Now, let's read.

I like to start by looking at what is behind the client. In this case, we have the Eight of Cups and the Hierophant. The Eight of Cups shows a figure who is walking away from something. This figure is leaving the comfort zone and heading off into an unknown destiny. Moriah has made some business changes in the last year. She is taking more time off to work on creative projects. She also let go of some work that she felt was "sucking her soul." This meant firing certain clients. Even though the money was good, the stress from these people was not worth it.

The Hierophant is the card of structure, teacher, and mentor. I asked Moriah if she had been studying something new or creating new policies. She said that she was learning a new technique, and part of the changes in her business meant raising her rates and establishing an application process for new clients so she could decide if they were a good fit. Some people balked at this procedure.

The mini-cross shows the Seven of Pentacles crossed by the Knight of Wands. It's interesting because the Seven of Pentacles means slow growth and reflection while the Knight is rarin' to go. This combination tells me that the lack of money coming in has perhaps made it hard for Moriah to move ahead with new projects. It's also forced her to take risks. Moriah said she had to put money on her credit card to cover some bills, which made her feel stressed.

The good news: Ten of Pentacles in the position that symbolizes her. For one, that tells me that Moriah has abundance consciousness. Even though her finances are tight at the moment, she knows that she can always make money. Moriah has a strong community and a loving family to draw positive inspiration from. This also tells me that her desire to make money isn't just for materialism but also because she wants to take good care of the people under her wings.

I jump to the Hopes and Fears position to see if there is a contradiction between these two cards. The Three of Cups and Ten of Pentacles are both cards of abundance. This reading reinforces her desire to be secure and abundant. There are no mixed signals here at all.

Her environment has the Strength card, a card that often indicates struggling to get a situation under control. Moriah again reiterated that using the credit cards was something she didn't want to do but had to so that she could keep things afloat.

The cards that symbolize the future are the Eight of Wands, Six of Pentacles, and King of Swords. I like to read these as a trio. Movement and news are coming. Something is about to change (Eight of Wands). Financial deals are coming through. People who need her work will be reaching out (Six of Pentacles). She'll be in control soon (King of Swords). The other way to look at these cards is possible help coming her way through a client. She may be landing a profitable contract soon.

Either way, the weeks that follow should find her getting right back on track. (And she did!)

Your turn: How would you interpret these cards? What advice would you give Moriah? How might you interpret the King of Swords? Is that her, or someone who might be influencing her situation? Journal your thoughts.

Reading Two: A General Outlook

This second reading is for Ronald, a middle-aged man who is in the midst of a divorce. Here are the cards:

- 1—Two of Cups

- 2—Hanged Man

- 3—Five of Swords

- 4—The Hermit

- 5—Queen of Wands

- 6—King of Pentacles reversed

- 7—Temperance reversed

- 8—Queen of Cups

- 9—The Fool

- 10—Nine of Wands

The presence of two reversals shows that some inner work needs to be done. But also what catches my eye are the two Queens and the Five of Swords. Immediately, I wonder if there has been infidelity. He confirms that, yes, there has been.

Now, let's do the reading.

The Five of Swords is the card of deception. It's a sign that something has gone drastically wrong in Ronald's life in the last year. A situation erupted, a storm came through, and feelings were hurt. Because the Five of Swords has three people in it, that also reinforces the infidelity interpretation.

The Hermit shows that he's pulled away from the situation to try to understand his role or figure out what he's doing—that time has given him a chance to reflect on what has happened. He needed to withdraw from the shit-show his life had become to get clear on what he wants.

The mini-cross contains the Two of Cups with the Hanged Man. Now that might say a sacrifice is being made for love. What could that sacrifice be? I look over to the King of Pentacles reversed and say that a financial sacrifice will need to be made. His situation might become costly.

Temperance reversed shows he's going back and forth, unable to make a decision. Because there are two Queens, this leads me to believe Ronald hasn't made up his mind between the two women in his life. The Queen of Cups in his environment is the partner at home. Obviously, there is still love present. They have children together, so there is definitely an emotional bond. The Queen of Wands shows the fire element; he has a passion for this person. I ask if the sex is better with the new person. He says yes.

In the Hopes and Fears position, he has the Fool. A desire to start a new life. Wanting to put the old baggage behind. When I look at that card and the Temperance reversed, I'm struck by the two Majors. That tells me that this is a crossroads in his life.

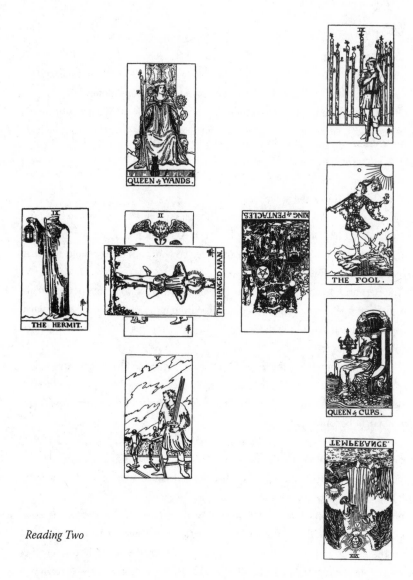

Reading Two

He wants to be free, but the Temperance reversed shows he's waffling. Again, the King of Pentacles reversed shows the potential loss of money is influencing his indecision. He might go back and forth between the two women for some time as a result.

The Nine of Wands rules the future. Fear of making a change. Setbacks. There may be other anxieties holding him in place too. The energy here is cowardly and sneaky. He might even be making underhanded financial moves to protect his money.

Of course, this reading got me curious. Was he playing games? What was up here? Ronald admitted that he had strayed on his marriage on other occasions, but he had always come back to his wife. The newest lover is exciting, and he feels a deeper connection with her, especially on a physical level. She also shares his love of the outdoor life, which his wife does not. He feels he has more in common with the new woman. But Ronald has quite a lot of money to lose because he does not have a prenuptial agreement with the wife, so he's trying to stall matters until he can find a way to reroute the cash. (By the way, it's not my job to judge that—just to read.) The cards show that this situation may play out for some time. The Hanged Man and Temperance reversed suggest everything is on hold while he sorts matters out.

Now, the presence of four Major Arcanas shows a karmic pattern here. I pull the cards out, and we look at them:

- Card 1: The Lesson—Hanged Man

- Card 2: The Current Position on the Karmic Path—The Hermit

- Card 3: The Direction Ahead on the Karmic Path—Temperance reversed

- Card 4 (and any additional cards): Reflection—The Fool

The lesson is about letting go. Something here seems to be buried. A part of Ronald's life is hung up, stuck, and unable to move.

The current position on the karmic path is the Hermit. He's learning a valuable lesson. Perhaps he's dealing with something internal, something that needs a tremendous amount of inner work to unravel.

The direction ahead on the karmic path is Temperance reversed—the standstill. Sorting matters out. There is a path behind him with a crown falling, which says he has to make peace with the past. Perhaps a past karmic situation.

Reflection is the Fool—a fresh start. Wanting to make a change. The desire to move forth, sans baggage. Not just his own, but perhaps something else.

Ronald reveals that when he was little, his father also cheated on his mother. His parents went through a nasty divorce, and his father played dirty, which ultimately led to Ronald's mother getting swindled out of money she needed and deserved. Although the children didn't go without, there was constant bickering around cash. His parents were in and out of the courts for years. Ronald was angry at his father for hurting his mother, whom he loved deeply (she passed recently). He also felt as though he could never please his father, who was a powerful and intimidating figure in his life.

Now here he is in a similar situation just like his father. This is bringing up a lot of old baggage. He doesn't want to be like his father, but he also doesn't want to be stuck in a marriage that no longer lights him up.

My recommendation was for some good long-term therapy to work through the daddy issues. A counselor could also help him make a decision out of integrity, one that felt fair to him and his wife should they decide to split up. This would undo the potential damage that hiding his money could do. Rather than repeat the sins of the father, Ronald is sitting on the fence because, on some level deep inside, he remembers how much his father hurt his mother, both emotionally and financially, and he doesn't want to do that to his wife.

I finished the reading by saying, "It's complicated." And he agreed. There are many levels of intense inner work that he needs to do to make a decision that feels healthy . . . and right.

I pulled one more card for guidance: the World. The World symbolizes a need to close a chapter. I saw that as probably his marriage (although it could be the other relationship). But it may also point to closing the karmic chapter with his father. Rather than following in his dad's footsteps, Ronald needs to break away from the pattern and do the right thing.

As of this writing, Ronald is still in the same situation. Like the Temperance reversed, he has not been able to make a move. Both women are still in his life, but he spends the majority of his time with his new love. And yes, Ronald's still trying to figure out his money situation. Has he worked on things with his father? Well, they get along, and on some level, he realizes that he's more like his father than he thought. This means there's not much progress in that situation either.

This was a challenging reading because, although the cards confirmed the situation and possibility of trouble, an alternate route was available. But that's the thing with tarot: we can see the potential, but sometimes people are stuck in their patterns, and in those cases, all we can do is mind our own karma and just read the cards.

Your turn: What are some other possible interpretations for those cards? What advice might you give Ronald? How would you feel if you gave this reading and found out a year later that this person was still in the same position? What cards might reflect that happening?

Tarotcise

Lay out Ronald's cards in a straight line. How does the story unfold? If you were writing a soap opera script, what might the story line look like?

Tarotcise

With the cards still in a horizontal line, do the Memento Tarotcise (see page 191). Start with the last card and read backward. What do you discover about Ronald's past decisions and how they are impacting his future? (Psst, Two of Cups sums it all up! The Nine of Wands shows uncertainty as the outcome, but we can trace Ronald's predicament back to meeting someone new.)

When you first begin to dip your toes in the tarot water, the Celtic Cross may seem intimidating. Don't give up! Again: practice makes perfect. Do this spread as often as you can—both for questions and general outlooks. Read for a variety of situations and people. Soon, your intuitive ticker tape will start clicking, and the information will spill out of you!

Fine-Tuning Your Intuitive Tarot Readings

So far we've covered the tarot and intuition basics. I've given you exercises to build your skills and confidence. I've shared my three favorite spreads for tapping in and delivering insightful readings. That's enough, right?

Nope.

In this chapter, I share all of my best tips and techniques to help you finesse your readings like a pro. Think of this part as the delicious cream cheese icing on the tarot cake. (Hmmm, I'm suddenly craving carrot cake for some reason.)

Numbers

Every single card in the tarot deck is numbered except for the Court cards. Those numbers are chosen with care. In fact, they hold meaning and can give clues about the nature of each card. For example, the Emperor is ruled by the number 4, which indicates stability. Consider how he sits on his stone throne with the mountain behind him, entirely in charge. Now, look at the Four of Pentacles. This figure holds tightly to a coin, balancing another on his head, each foot firmly planted on another. Like the Emperor, he's in control, too, but in a different way. One creates security for the realm, whereas the other puts coins away for a rainy day.

See how that works?

Here are the general meanings for each number:

- 0—Infinity, limitless, nothingness

- 1 (Ace)—Beginning, a fresh start

- 2—Connection, decision, union, duality

- 3—Creativity, birth, joy

- 4—Stability, security

- 5—Change, conflict, disruption

- 6—Harmony, balance, giving and receiving, support

- 7—Struggle, knowledge, challenge

- 8—Achievement, success, proficiency

- 9—Completion, fulfillment, maturity

- 10—Ending and new beginning all wrapped up in one

When you combine the numbers with the suits, you can quickly determine what the card might mean. For example, the Ace of Wands might symbolize a new venture, whereas the Ten of Wands might indicate that you're coming to the end of a project or period of hard labor.

Knowing the numbers can help jog your tarot brain when it goes blank. You might be wondering about the Majors, which also have numbers. As I mentioned previously, the same rules apply.

For double-digit cards, you have two options: first, you can reduce the number by adding the two numbers. Using the Death card as an example, 13 becomes 1 + 3 = 4. This tells you that there is an element of security in this card too. As my friend Joe used to say: "The only thing that is unchanging is change."

Second, interpret each number separately. In the case of Death, 13 becomes 1, which indicates a new beginning, and 3, which is creativity. The traditional meaning of this card is change and endings, so breaking down 13 to a 1 and a 3 would mean that a new beginning is on the way, and something else is being birthed.

Here's one more cool example to ponder: The Hanged Man is ruled by the number 12. If you add that up, you get 3, which is attributed to creativity. Three also governs the Empress, which is the card of motherhood. The Hanged Man is the position that one assumes in the birth canal, with a golden halo symbolizing the crowning moment.

As the Hanged Man makes his sacrifice, he becomes reborn. As you can see, these two cards have way more in common than you might think at first glance.

The numbers also come in handy when you explore the patterns in a spread. If you have a bunch of Aces, you can determine there is a fresh start ahead. Many Fives would suggest a chaotic, unpredictable time. Always pay attention to multiples of anything, including the numbers. They are vital clues that will help piece together the tarot story.

My friend Pleasant Gehman shared a numerology technique with me on my podcast that you might want to test out. Add all the numbers present in a tarot spread and reduce the sum. That final number is the overarching theme. Here's an example of how that might look: Let's say you're asking about a new job. The cards you get are Judgement (20), Three of Swords, Eight of Pentacles, and the Hierophant reversed (5). You add up 2 + 0 + 3 + 8 + 5 = 18. Eighteen is associated with the Moon, which signals change and uncertainty. Reduce it further, and you get 9, the number of completion. Judging by the nature of the cards, you might conclude that the job will have ups and downs and may come to an end at some point, especially if the querent doesn't like to follow the rules.

Tarotcise

Shuffle the cards and do a three-card reading on any question you like. Using Pleasant's technique, add the numbers. Reduce the number further if need be. What themes can you pick up with that final number? How does it play out with the cards you pulled?

Timing

"When will things happen?" Folks want exact timelines, but that isn't always easy to determine. Timing is tricky and not foolproof! At best, you're guesstimating when something might go down. Although you may hit the proverbial nail on the head, often events will unfold slower or quicker than you might see in the cards.

When it comes to picking a time frame, I prefer to go with my gut. However, I also have a few simple methods that can help find possible dates. I always look at the final card as the "when." Is it a Minor? The seasons rule. Major? Astrology is your friend.

Minors for Timing

Each suit in the Minors corresponds to a season:

- Wands—Spring (Aries marks the beginning of spring; hence, we start with the Fire element.)

- Cups—Summer (Cancer marks the beginning of summer; hence, summer is the Water element.)

- Swords—Fall (Libra marks the beginning of fall, which makes swords the Fall element.)

- Pentacles—Winter (Capricorn marks the beginning of winter, so winter is Earth element.)

Let's say you're asking about when you might be able to sell your house. The card you pull is the Four of Wands. This card might suggest springtime. If you get the Five of Swords, you will wait until fall.

Majors for Timing

A few Major Arcana are connected to zodiac signs. If your reading finishes with one of these, you can use the time the Sun is in that sign for predicting an outcome.

- The Emperor—Aries (March 21–April 19)

- The Hierophant—Taurus (April 20–May 20)

- The Lovers—Gemini (May 21–June 20)

- The Chariot—Cancer (June 21–July 22)

- Strength—Leo (July 23–August 22)

- The Hermit—Virgo (August 23–September 22)

- Justice—Libra (September 23–October 22)

- Death—Scorpio (October 23–November 21)

- Temperance—Sagittarius (November 22–December 21)

- The Devil—Capricorn (December 22–January 19)

- The Star—Aquarius (January 20–February 18)

- The Moon—Pisces (February 19–March 20)

Using a previous example, if the Strength card were pulled instead of the Four of Wands, you might be looking at "Leo season," which would be the period of July 23–August 22. The Moon? You're looking at Pisces, which means the home would be selling around February 19–March 20.

My friend Al Juarez likes to look for clues in the cards themselves. The snowy setting in the Five of Pentacles can suggest winter, while the pumpkins in the Three of Cups might mean October. The Fool could indicate New Year's Day, while the Empress might be Mother's Day. Use your imagination here and let the vibrant imagery of the cards speak!

If you're not sure when things might play out, it's okay to say, "I don't know." It's also perfectly fine to give generous time frames if you're feeling a bit unsure.

With practice, you'll get more accurate and may even develop your own method. That being said, if you're not comfortable giving dates and times, don't. It's not mandatory.

Tarotcise

 Turn on the news. Find a developing story, one that may be ongoing. Shuffle the cards and ask when the situation will be resolved. Lay three cards in the Past Present Future spread. What does the Future card say about when the situation might come to a conclusion? Write down your answers, and then wait and see when it manifests.

Significators

A *significator* is a card that is consciously chosen to represent the querent (or a person they are asking about). Some spreads may require a significator, but often it is optional. I rarely use them because I feel that the card that represents the querent at the time of the reading will show up after we begin laying them down.

Most of the time, Court cards are chosen for significators. While there are traditional gender meanings for each Court card, I prefer to keep them neutral when doing a reading. As I mentioned in the section about Courts, not everyone will identify with the gender assigned at birth; plus, people can flip between being any of the Court members depending on the situation.

For example, although I identify as a woman, when I'm asking a question about business, I might choose a King to represent myself.

Before you pick a Court, a good practice would be to ask people what pronoun they prefer. This way, you can ensure they get one that they can relate to.

The Court figures are

- Page—Child, young person, or a person who identifies as a young female

- Knight—Person who identifies as a young male eighteen to thirties

- Queen—Person who identifies as a woman eighteen plus

- King—Person who identifies as a mature male forty plus

Once you've determined the appropriate Court member, use the elements to determine which suit:

- Cups—Water signs: Cancer, Scorpio, Pisces

- Wands—Fire signs: Aries, Leo, Sagittarius

- Swords—Air signs: Gemini, Libra, Aquarius

- Pentacles—Earth signs: Taurus, Virgo, Capricorn

For example:

- A person who identifies as a young male and is a Cancer would be a Knight of Cups.

- A person who identifies as a woman and is a Virgo would be the Queen of Pentacles.

- A person who identifies as a student and is a Gemini would be the Page of Swords.

- A person who identifies as a mature male and is a Sagittarius would be the King of Wands.

This is my most trusted way of picking a good significator.

The Major Arcana can also be used as a significator. In this case, you would use only the ones that are associated with the zodiac signs:

- The Emperor—Aries

- The Hierophant—Taurus

- The Lovers—Gemini

- The Chariot—Cancer

- Strength—Leo

- The Hermit—Virgo

- Justice—Libra

- Death—Scorpio

- Temperance—Sagittarius

- The Devil—Capricorn

- The Star—Aquarius

- The Moon—Pisces

One last method is to use the Birth card. Birth cards are based on the work of Angeles Arrien and Mary K. Greer. In fact, Greer wrote an entire book on the subject called *Who Are You in the Tarot?* I highly recommend that book if you want to use this method. Here's how it works:

Add the numbers in your date of birth. Reduce the numbers and find the Major Arcana that connects with it. For example, Barack Obama was born August 4, 1961.

- $8 + 4 + 1 + 9 + 6 + 1 = 29.$

- $2 + 9 = 11.$

The number 11 corresponds to Justice, which means this might be the card you choose for his significator. Keep in mind that 11 can be reduced further to 2, which is associated with the High Priestess. If he prefers, he could choose that card instead of Justice.

Tarotcise

Use each method to determine a significator for yourself. Which one makes the most sense for you at this time? Can you see another time when the other cards might work better? Journal your thoughts about different significators at different times in your life.

Missing Suits

Pay close attention to missing suits, for they hold clues too. For example, if someone is asking about love, and no Cups cards are present, that might be a sign of relationship issues. Perhaps the querent is lacking a connection with their partner. Or maybe they are emotionally unavailable. See how that works?

Missing suits are especially relevant for a general outlook. A missing suit indicates clue areas that may be unimportant or perhaps something the querent may be ignoring. For example, if the missing suit is the Major Arcana, that might indicate the current focus is on the mundane, day-to-day part of life. If there are no Pentacles, money may not be the pressing issue.

Keep in mind that some folks want a general outlook and get upset when the one thing they really want to focus on doesn't show up in the cards.

For example, I read for a woman, and zero Cups cards were in the spread. Of course, that made her anxious because she was hoping to see a romantic forecast. Crestfallen, she assumed this meant that she would not meet anyone. I asked her if there was a lot of drama at work (she had a ton of Wands and Swords). She admitted that things were dicey on the job as of late, and she had been working overtime. That left little time for love.

We did another spread focused on romance, and the cards showed potential (yay for Cups cards), but once again, the majority of suits present were Wands and Pentacles. It became apparent that she needed to make some changes around her job if she was going to have any bandwidth left to pursue relationships.

A few months later, this client returned and announced that she took a new, more flexible position, and she had begun dating a new woman. The next spread we did? Ace of Cups, baby. Yay for tarot!

Tarotcise

 The next time you do a reading, begin by looking at what's missing first. Take a moment to journal what that might mean. How does it impact the reading?

Pay Attention to How the Cards Are Interacting and Flowing

Do the cards face each other or face away? For example, if you pull the Queen of Wands followed by the Queen of Cups, they would face each other. This arrangement would show interaction is happening.

Perhaps this spread could indicate a meeting of the minds or two friends coming together to plan an event. But what if we reversed the order? If we switched these Queens, they would look in two different directions. That could imply that the people involved are not able to see eye to eye. In a question about relationships, this arrangement could suggest that they want different things.

How do the cards flow? Are there specific themes that dominate the reading? Or is it a mishmash of different suits, reversals, and Courts? Take a deep breath and try to find the patterns and where the energy seems to be moving.

Always look at the final card and then back to the beginning. The likely outcome shows where the querent is heading, and the rest of the cards will show the journey to that point.

Background Noise

Be sure to check out the "background noise" in your tarot images. Often, readers are more focused on the central figures, but if you look at backgrounds, you can see many clues and rich symbols that add depth to your interpretations.

For example, notice the abundant wheat harvest at the feet of the Empress. What wealth has she created? How about smoke billowing out of the Tower? What is "going up in smoke"? Or the storm clouds in the Five of Swords? What energy do they convey?

Tarotcise

 Go through all the cards in the deck and study the backgrounds. What's going on? Jot down some ideas for each backdrop in your journal. Doing so can broaden your interpretations and your tarot vocabulary!

Gestures

Pay close attention to the hand gestures in each of the cards. Notice the defensive posture of the Page of Swords as he raises the sword in a gesture of protection. Observe the jnana mudra on the Ten of Swords (jnana mudra is a yogic hand position for wisdom). Look at the gesture of offering in each of the Aces. And pay attention to the benediction in the hands of the Hierophant. What clues do they give you about these cards?

The Page of Swords could be interpreted as a need to protect your turf, the hand in the Ten of Swords might suggest the wisdom that comes after loss, the Ace of Cups could be the offer of love, and the Hierophant could be an indication of a blessing granted. Gestures tell a lot.

What's around the Card?

Another thing to keep in mind is the surrounding cards because they can impact the reading. For example, let's say you're asking about romance, and you pull the Lovers. Yay, right? Perhaps. But what if the other cards are the Five of Swords, the Devil, and the Hanged Man?

Well, now, we see a relationship that could be full of drama and deception. Perhaps there is a karmic lesson to be resolved in this pairing. All of those cards change the nature of the Lovers, which we often assume to be a happy relationship omen. Every card impacts the other.

Progressions

You'll also want to notice if the cards show a sequential order, or what I call "progressions." If they do, that indicates the situation is moving along.

Let me give you an example. Let's say your first card is the Two of Pentacles. If the next cards are the Three of Cups and the Five of Pentacles, we can see a situation is moving forward. If the order were reversed, it would symbolize that you may be going back to the drawing board.

One of my favorite progressions is with the Courts. If a reading shows a Page, followed by a Knight, Queen, and King, a situation is developing from beginning to completion. This progression is especially auspicious when the Courts are in the same suit. For example, if they were all from the Pentacles suit, they might indicate a money-making idea that becomes a successful venture.

The Full House

Speaking of all the Courts, if all four members of the Court show up, I call it a "full house," an indicator that many people are contributing to the situation. If all four members of the Court also are from each suit, it's a sign that you have everything you need and all the right people in place to help you achieve your goal.

For example, if you're asking a question about your job and the cards pulled are Page of Cups, Knight of Pentacles, Queen of Swords, and King of Wands, you've got every person and all the suits. They don't need to be in order like a progression; they just need to be represented.

As Above, So Below

I mentioned this technique briefly as a Tarotcise in the "How to Shuffle" section, but it's worth repeating: peek at the card on the bottom of the deck before interpreting. This card can give a hint as to what's on the querent's mind, which is helpful for general outlooks. It can also reveal something that they are not sharing.

For example, once I was reading for a woman who had the Three of Cups on the bottom. The rest of the reading showed significant drama in her personal life and a situation that would come to a head soon. She shifted in her seat uncomfortably. Finally, she said she was thinking of leaving her spouse because she had met a new man. She didn't want to mention that because she was afraid I would judge her.

Stalker Cards

Sometimes it seems the same card comes up again and again. I call those "stalker" cards, as in that particular card is trying to get your attention! If you find one keeps turning up in your readings, even readings for other people, make a note of it. What is it trying to tell you? How is it showing up in your life? Is there a lesson you're still learning?

Recently, I was doing a book signing, and two friends were standing by my table chatting while people came up to meet me and my coauthor, Shaheen Miro. I pulled out my baby tarot deck and was allowing people to choose a card at random for a quick mini-read. Everyone seemed to pull Major Arcanas. When my friends walked away briefly, everyone started getting Minors. As soon as my friends returned, once again, it was Major after Major! Obviously, the tarot was trying to send these two a message!

Jumpers

Sometimes a card will seem to leap out of a deck when you're shuffling. My friend Paige Zaferiou calls these "jumpers." These cards are trying to get your attention. A saying that I like is "What falls to the floor comes to the door," meaning that any cards that fall out while shuffling are situations that might be coming into the querent's life soon.

When one card falls out, I put it aside facedown and come back to it after I've read the other cards. You might choose to do this too. Or you may feel like taking a glance and putting it back into the deck.

Keep in mind that some people will do everything they can to create a jumper. I have two clients like this. They shuffle as sloppily as they can, and when a card falls out, they can barely contain their grin as they say, "What does *that* mean?" It takes every ounce of my being to keep a straight face as I say, "It means you're a clumsy shuffler." There are always those types who want their readings to be spooky or special. Never entertain folks who play that game.

Help! I've Drawn a Blank!

Nothing is more frustrating than turning over a card and getting nothing. You panic and begin sweating while this dialogue runs through your head: "Do I look at the book? No . . . that wouldn't be right. Come on, brain, give me a clue! D'oh!"

I've been there. For the record, even seasoned pros still draw a blank from time to time. It just happens.

There are a few ways to deal with drawing a blank:

1. If you're new, feel free to pull out a book and find an interpretation. That may jog your intuition and get you back on the right tarot track.

2. Skip the card and move on to another. In the case of a large spread, this approach is perfectly acceptable. Come back to it and see if anything arises.

3. Start describing the card. Doing this will often lead to an interpretation. For example, let's look at the Ace of Pentacles. "I see a large hand holding a coin. The hand seems to be coming out of the sky. There is a path with flowers leading to a gate. There seems to be a big garden beyond that path." Interpretation: "An offer comes out of the blue that leads to an exciting new path." *Bada bing*!

4. Consider the question asked. Was it valid? Were you uncomfortable with it? If you are feeling some type of way about a subject or even the person sitting before you, that could get in the way. The same thing happens if you're invested in the outcome. Having an emotional stake in the reading can interfere with your intuition, and suddenly, you're blank! Centering can help, but more importantly, if you cannot be objective, now may not be the right time, or you may not be the right person for the job.

5. Sometimes, for no reason at all, you just get nothing. That happens. The answer may not be there, or it may not be yours to answer. Send the querent to a different reader and pack up your cards. You cannot read for everyone or every situation. And that's perfectly fine.

Tarotcise

Think of a question and then pull a card. Write down every detail that you can find in the card. From there, see what interpretations you can find.

Help! I'm in a Tarot Rut!

Getting in a tarot rut happens more often than you'd like. Every tarot reader at one time or another, especially high-volume readers, experiences burnout. When that happens, your deck seems to be giving you nothing at all, no matter how hard you try. You might even find that you're giving the same old rote meanings for every reading. Worse yet, your intuition seems to be on a permanent vacation.

You can take a time-out (which is sometimes necessary). Or you can do this one simple thing: pick a new deck—preferably one you've never worked with before, one that is utterly unfamiliar to you. Using a new deck will wake up your tarot brain. The reason: new images force your intuition to get to work. Think about it: When someone wears the same suit day in and day out, we become accustomed to it. But when that person shows up in brand-new duds, it captures our attention. We notice. Same with tarot.

Tarotcise

Buy or borrow a new deck. Make sure it's one that you have never used before. Better yet, if you're a Rider-Waite-Smith person, get your hands on a Marseilles or Thoth deck. Do a reading and see how your mind has to search for new interpretations. How does it feel to work with a different set of cards?

Tarotcise

Grab a deck of playing cards. Try doing a reading with them. Can you find interpretations with an ordinary non-tarot deck?

Can My Friend Sit with Me?

Some people want their reading with a buddy on hand. If you're comfortable with that, by all means, go for it. But do know that sometimes the other person can impact the reading.

For example, if the friend sits at the table and interjects, it can throw off the reading. If they are the curious sort who never had a reading and want to treat this as some sort of "ooh, let me see if I want to try this one day," that can make you nervous. Also, sometimes shit comes up in a reading that perhaps the querent doesn't want revealed. If you see something that may be delicate, you might feel uncomfortable saying anything in front of the other person. In that case, the awkward situation can lead to a stiff reading and one that, while it may be entertaining to the person sitting in, isn't helpful for the querent.

That Reading Was Boring AF!

Sometimes a tarot reading doesn't have a lot of wow power. Instead of a glamorous future with some underworld spy or the wife of a close friend à la Carly Simon, the cards show mundane life with the same-old, same-old.

I'm a practical gal. When I get a tarot reading, I expect it to be boring because I live a no-drama life. But some people get disappointed if the reading doesn't show new, exciting developments. I have to remind them that the cards are showing that everything is alright. Sometimes life is just okay—and that's not only perfectly fine but also a good thing.

That Reading Was Totally Wrong!

Nobody ever likes hearing this, but if you read tarot for any amount of time, at some point, someone is going to let you know that "nothing came true." There are a few reasons why this can happen:

1. You're still new at this. If that's the case, don't take that criticism to heart. Every skill (and yes, tarot and intuition are both skills) takes time to develop. Rarely, can someone just nail it right out of the tarot box.

2. You weren't comfortable with the questions. If I'm troubled with the questions posed, I might feel timid. This doesn't bode well for an accurate reading. I have learned that it's better to say that I'm not down with this line of questioning rather than try to wing my way through it. For example, when people ask about gambling, I refuse to engage. I have a personal prejudice against gambling, and that colors my ability to be objective.

3. The person wasn't receptive. If you are reading for a skeptic, they will be sure to make it as hard as possible because they want you to be wrong. Even if you're

totally dead-on, they will come back and let you know that it didn't work. Those types are never out to get a helpful reading. Their only goal is to discredit you. If you sense the person is not open or is playing games, put your cards away.

4. You misinterpreted the cards. This is often the case. The cards may be right on the money, but your interpretations weren't. This reason doesn't usually come to light until later reflection. You can learn a lot by revisiting these "wrong" readings and seeing where your interpretation might have gone sideways.

5. You were too invested in the outcome. When you have a personal stake in the outcome, you cannot be objective. You'll either see what you want . . . or what you don't want. I've done this too and have learned that when I can't be objective, it's time to hire another pro!

6. Sometimes you'll read for a person who thinks that life "happens to them." They will come to the reading hoping you'll deliver the news they want, and then they'll sit back and do nothing. I find this usually happens in love readings. The person wants to know if they'll meet someone, and when the cards show a yes, they assume it's going to happen without their involvement. Tarot is not a passive act. It shows the possibility, but you still have to do your part. These are the hardest people to read for. No matter how you try to explain their role, they just don't want to believe that they are responsible for their future success . . . or lack thereof. They prefer to blame the cards instead.

7. Sometimes a person either doesn't understand the reading or interprets your interpretation differently. For example, I read for a woman and turned over the Five of Pentacles in the "recent past" position. I said she had been unemployed not that long ago. She got mad and told me I was wrong. About ten minutes later, she said she was recently laid off from her job. This got me a bit pissy, and I said, "That's what I just said." Her reply? "Oh, I don't think being laid off is the same thing as being unemployed." Urgh.

These are the main culprits for the wrong readings. But do know that everyone has an off day. You can't possibly see everything for everyone. And that's okay.

Sometimes There Are No Answers

It happens to the best of us. The cards show nothing, nada, zilch. The future is a blank slate. You're blanker than a freshly scrubbed chalkboard. Even the information that is coming through feels vague.

Sometimes there are no answers. You can't possibly see everything. No one has that power. In the case of a reading when you don't see a definitive outcome, it is better to be honest about that and to give any pertinent information around the question you are receiving.

For example, a woman wanted to know when she would sell her house. The cards showed a lousy market, and the outcome was the Moon, which can mean a lack of clarity or unforeseen problems. I told her that I felt she would sell the house, but I didn't have any information about when. I couldn't see a thing. She didn't like that, but it was better than me trying to fish out some bullshit answer that wasn't there. Needless to say, the house sat on the market for months without a nibble. Frustrated, she took it off the market. The last time we spoke, she was thinking about putting it up for sale again. This time, the cards showed a happy ending.

Another woman I read for was planning to move to Arizona to be with her boyfriend. She wanted to know when it was going to happen. The card that came up was the Eight of Wands reversed. I said the move was going to be delayed due to an obstacle. "How delayed?" I didn't know. The next time I saw her, she said that she never moved because she discovered he was seeing another person.

One more story: I was reading at a party when a woman asked about a trip she was planning. There was that Eight of Wands reversed again! I told her that her journey would be delayed, and she'd have trouble getting off the ground. She said that everything was meticulously planned, and no way would this happen. "What would cause the delay?" I pulled cards and got nothing. I told her I didn't know, and perhaps I was wrong. A few months later, she saw me and said her trip did indeed get canceled. I asked what happened. She said the trip was scheduled for September 11, 2001. That was the day the Twin Towers were attacked and all flights got canceled.

Can I Ask the Question Again If I Didn't Like the Outcome?

Ah, it is tempting to ask a question again if you don't like the way it rolls out. I'm not a fan of beating a dead tarot horse. Get your answer and be done with it. Maybe make some changes in your life and revisit the card again at a later date. Other than that, a do-over or "tarot mulligan" isn't recommended. It usually leads to mixed messages, and in my experience, it also makes my tarot cards grouchy.

I have met people who will go from reader to reader to get the answer they want. They are often quick to demand a refund or leave a poor review when they don't get the shiny outcome they desire.

Years ago, I read for one such woman who inquired about an old love. She wanted to know if he would return. The cards showed a firm no. She said, "All of the other readers I have talked to over the years told me he would. You're the only one who didn't." I asked her how long she's been getting these readings and waiting on this dude. "Twenty years."

In other words, for the last two decades, she has been told that he would come back, but nothing happened, and here she was with a different reader hoping to get that same answer. On some level, she must have known that this situation was never going to work, but these readings fed into her fantasies. Needless to say, she got mad at me and gave me a nasty review. I have no idea if he ever came back or if she's still visiting those readers who told her he would.

What to Do If the Outcome Is Unfavorable?

Again, you do not want to keep pulling cards until you see a rosy future. Instead, I recommend picking one to three cards for advice. This approach takes the reading in an empowering direction and puts your future in your hands (or the hands of the sitter if you're reading for someone else). After all, your decisions help write your destiny. You have agency, and your reading should always make you feel that way.

A short advice reading is the wisest practice when the outcome isn't positive. I usually pull three additional cards for guidance when the reading ends on a sour note. This reminds the sitter that they have options and can change the course.

Also, you should never end a reading on a negative note, no matter what cards come up. You do not want people walking away from your tarot table feeling hopeless.

Instead, you want to make sure they feel inspired and empowered, no matter what the circumstance may be or the cards pulled.

You must choose your words with great care and be mindful about giving absolutes ("you'll definitely lose your job!"). Be honest about what you see, but then follow my advice and pull additional cards for guidance.

You'll need to be especially mindful when reading for parents of young children. If you see something negative in the cards, you do not wish to cause undue worry for the parent. (Psst . . . you can be wrong too.)

Recently, I spent a whole day consoling a friend who had received a frightening reading. The person implied her eight-year-old daughter would have "a hard life" and encounter many struggles. The tarot reader stated this as a fact and didn't give any solutions for the mother. Needless to say, she was crushed, and I ended up having to undo the damage that this other person caused.

We looked at what problems her child might face and how she, as the mother, could guide her in the best way possible. This is the proper way to handle a reading about a child if the cards are tricky.

Always remember your words matter. Carefully consider the ramifications of the information delivered. You cannot predict how people may react or what they will do after the reading. Still, you can certainly do your part to steer things in a productive, healthy, and hopeful direction.

At the end of the day, think about how you want people to feel when they work with you. Let that guide your words.

I'd like to finish this chapter by saying that sometimes life isn't fair and situations are not easily resolved. For some folks, circumstances may be severe, and they may need additional resources to make a change. While a tarot reading can be an ally, seeking other help may be necessary. In those situations, you'll want to refer them to the proper professionals.

More Tarotcises!

I've got a few more Tarotcises up my sleeve for you! Try them out and have fun with them. But never underestimate the playful nature of these little tarot experiments. Each one serves a purpose and will only help you become a better, faster, and more confident reader.

Built for Speed

This simple Tarotcise helps you bypass that part of your brain that wants to rely on the standard interpretations. It works best with two people. You'll need one of those little hourglasses that you might find in a board game.

One person shuffles the cards and pulls one off the top of the deck. The hourglass is turned upside down. Without thinking too deeply about the meaning, the other person starts interpreting the card as fast as they can. When the sand runs out on the timer, throw down another card, turn the hourglass upside down, and move on. And so on.

Reporter

Grab your favorite tarot deck and randomly pull a card. Now, pretend that you're a reporter for a famous newspaper, and you need to write a news flash based on this card. Get creative and have fun with this!

Example: Three of Wands—"Elton John is getting ready to launch his next tour. This is going to be his biggest one yet. Sir Elton plans on sailing around the world and performing in every dock."

Guessing Games

The next time you are out and about on your errands, notice people around you. Without interacting, what is the first Court card that comes to mind? Go ahead and make a snap judgement. It's all good.

Next, initiate a conversation and see if the person matches up with your first impression. For example, I met a woman the other day at the coffee shop (the best place for this Tarotcise, in my opinion). Right off the bat, I thought: Queen of Cups.

A quick little hello at the cream station, and her feisty nature was apparent. Whoops—Queen of Wands! It's incredible how many times I am right on with my snap judgements, but when I'm wrong, that gives me a chance to analyze my initial impressions.

In this case, it was the soft look in her eyes that made me think Cups. But a few words later and I saw the fire! Keep in mind that people can be any member of the Court, depending on the day. Try this one out and see what you learn about your impressions and what Court card energy people may be taking on.

Witness

Being able to picture all the details in a card will help you be a better tarot reader. I can visualize and describe each card in the Rider-Waite-Smith deck down to the finest detail.

Here's a Tarotcise to play: Pick your favorite deck. Pull a card randomly from the deck and take a minute to study the card. Turn the card facedown and then draw the card from memory as if you were doing a police sketch. Try to get as many details as you can. Give yourself two minutes, maximum. Finally, turn the card over and see how many details you got right. Are you a good tarot witness?

You Oughta Be in Pictures

Every movie director uses a storyboard as a visual organizer for preparing a film. Create your own using tarot!

Begin by creating an outline for a story. Now, choose tarot cards for each important scene or turning point. Lay them out, and then, with the cards as your images, fine-tune your story. Share it with someone you love (kids love this sort of thing).

Extra credit: use your camera phone and create a little film. Lay out the cards in order and begin filming with the first card. As the story moves along, move your camera to the next card and so on.

This Tarotcise will help you learn how the cards can work together to tell a story.

Lights, camera—*TAROT!*

Set the Stage

Think of a setting—any setting. What tarot cards might best illustrate that setting?

For example, choose a hospital. You might pick the Nine of Swords to represent a patient, King of Swords or Queen of Swords to represent a surgeon, Strength to describe a nurse, Chariot for the ambulance, Three of Cups for the return home. Got it?

Try this out with all sorts of different settings: a picnic (Queen of Pentacles might be the woman who brings the best fried chicken to the event!), a church (Hierophant time!), a funeral, etc. Make this a game, but you'll also see that these are patterns that may one day show up in a reading.

Behind the Scenes

What might be going on behind the scenes in some of these pictures?

The High Priestess. The walls of the city in the Four of Wands. The town the Chariot is leaving. Did you ever wonder what is going on in the background? Journal about what is going on behind the scenes.

Be curious. Let your imagination contemplate these scenes. Make your journal entry as vivid as possible. Tell the story of what might be happening in the backdrop. You might just discover some new interpretations!

Quoted

Pull a card and find a quote that best sums it up.

Example: Seven of Wands: "When we least expect it, life sets us a challenge to test our courage and willingness to change; at such a moment, there is no point in pretending that nothing has happened or in saying that we are not yet ready. The challenge will not wait. Life does not look back. A week is more than enough time for us to decide whether or not to accept our destiny."—Paulo Coelho

This is a fun way to add some new insights to your interpretations!

Musical Cards

Shuffle your deck and pull a card randomly. What is the first song that comes to your mind? If each tarot card had a theme song, what would it be?

Next, write a haiku or rap for each tarot card.

Pictures

I love taking photos of things that remind me of tarot cards. With the advent of smart-phones, I can click away whenever I'm inspired. For example, I've taken pics of a large scales statue in Portland for Justice, a fortune-teller's shop for the High Priestess, a sign for a restaurant called The Three Cups. You can find tarot photo inspiration all over your world . . . because tarot depicts daily life. Look for the tarot images around you.

Talking about the Weather

Namely, let's talk about the weather in the tarot cards. Look closely at your deck and see what clues the weather in the background might give for interpretations. For example, the storm clouds in the Five of Swords show trouble, while the bright yellow in the Three of Wands suggests optimism. Go through your deck and make notes. If you were a meteorologist, what might you predict based on the tarot weather?

Mad Men

Pretend that you are a marketing whiz, and you have to write an ad or tagline (or both) for each tarot card.

Example: Ace of Cups—"Drink up! If you're thirsty for love, the Ace of Cups will quench that thirst once and for all. This cup is flowing with new bubbly stuff sure to please—I'm talkin' love, baby. Pop that cork and take a swig!"

Different Venues

Explore reading tarot in different venues and see if the energy feels different for you. For example, you might want to try reading in a coffee shop, the beach, at a family barbecue, or in the park with a blanket on the earth.

What feels better? What other energies might you be noticing? Does one environment feel stronger . . . or more distracting? Pay close attention to how different settings work (or don't work) for you.

Guess the Plot

Guessing the plot is an excellent way to build your prediction chops.

Pick your favorite television show character (I'll use Jaime Lannister from *Game of Thrones* as my example). Now, shuffle the cards, focusing on what your character's next big move or plotline might be. Pick one card, turn it over, and make your prediction. Then . . . wait until the next episode and see what actually happens. Were you right? Might there be a new way to look at that card?

I pulled the Seven of Swords for Jaime Lannister. This tells me that he may find himself having to exit a situation quickly to avoid danger, or he may do something extremely underhanded and then have to go on the run! Either way, he's sneaking off and getting away with something.

What happened: He ditched Brienne of Tarth and went running back to Cersei like the rogue he was!

As you can see, there are many ways to play with your tarot cards. Have fun and keep shuffling!

Going Pro

At some point, you may find that you're adept. In fact, you may get so good that people want to pay you for your talent. You might be inspired to start a tarot business. Yay! The world needs more good readers as tarot becomes more popular.

I get a lot of questions from people who want to turn their tarot hobby into a lucrative business. In this chapter, I pull back the High Priestess curtain and reveal the things you need to know before you hang out your lantern.

Let's start off with a reality check:

The Good

1. Tarot is an act of service. There is nothing better than helping people move through their trials and tribulations.

2. Starting a tarot business doesn't take a lot of capital. In fact, I started with nothing more than a deck and some business cards. You can create a website cheaply or for no cost. At this time, most social media platforms are free too, which means your marketing budget doesn't have to be significant.

3. A tarot business can be fun! Parties and events can bring you into contact with interesting people. You can wear a costume if you'd like (every day is Halloween for tarot pros!).

4. Tax deduction: you might be able to write off every tarot book and deck, as well as those tarot conferences. Business expense! Yay!

5. Tarot is more popular than ever, which means you can find plenty of work out there.

6. Back in the day, we had to hustle hard for business. With the advent of the internet, you can reach people on a global level, and that ups your chances of success!

The Bad

1. The hours can be *long*. Sure, it looks as though I'm working a few hours here and there, but the truth is, most days are ten hours. That's not just client work. It's also marketing, writing, doing paperwork, paying bills, learning new technology, and so on. Self-employment is *rarely* a ticket to freedom despite what some may say.

2. If tarot is your only source of income, you'll have to get used to an unsteady income. That can be terrifying, especially when you consider that you'll need to put money aside for taxes, health insurance, and retirement. You will have to manage your money smartly.

3. Taxes. Oof. This aspect scares many well-intentioned tarot pros from going all the way. You have to pay taxes on that money you're making. There is no way to avoid this.

4. You might just get flack from your family if you want to do this.

5. The learning never ends. Tarot requires consistent practice, much like musicians have to do with their instruments.

The Ugly

1. You will deal with some difficult people. Folks who want to test you. Freebie seekers who play on your sympathies. Rude types who want to attack you for just showing up and doing the work. People who are unstable, unreasonable, and looking to take it out on you. Every business has this issue. Tarot isn't immune from jerks.

2. You may be subjected to big fines, depending on where you are located. There are antiquated laws on the books in some parts of the world that frown on "fortune-telling." This could cost you.

3. The work can be dangerous. You'll want to rethink allowing strangers in your home or reading at a drunken gathering. I've got lots of horror stories from the time I got stuck reading for a gang leader to the time the abusive ex-husband of a client tried to use a fake name to set up an appointment because he wanted to "teach me a lesson."

4. You will encounter both skeptics and religious types who want to discredit you . . . loudly. These are the folks who will attack you online, troll you, speak down to you, tell others how fake you are, and do whatever they can to bring you down. You'll have to develop a thick skin.

5. Some clients will ignore your boundaries. They will expect you to drop everything and read for them—even if it's on the weekend. When you don't, they become abusive.

6. You may encounter jealous peers who throw shade at you, local readers who undercut your prices, and scam artists who rip off clients. When you get lumped in with the latter, it hurts. Oh, and you'll have to clean up their messes too.

7. You'll also have dreadfully slow periods when no work comes in at all, followed by a deluge of requests that make you feel as if you cannot keep up. Do not throw in the towel. Ride the wave.

Get the picture? While doing the work you were meant to do is exciting, tarot work, like any job, also comes with plenty of challenges along the way. Those who are called to this work will plow on, good times and bad, lessons learned along the way. But for many, it's too much. I've seen many well-intentioned folks come into this work only to run away screaming.

If I haven't scared you off, let's get down to the basics.

When Should You Start?

I read tarot for ten years before it became my profession. That decade gave me a solid foundation in both tarot and people skills, which made my transition to a full-time pro rather painless. I knew what I was doing.

Too often, people go pro before they are ready. The reason is usually that their motivation is skewed. They assume that tarot is easy money, and after playing around with the cards for a few months, think, "What the hell . . . I might as well buy a deck and make a living doing this." If that's your mindset, you'll quickly learn that it's not easy money. It's the most challenging work I've ever done in my life.

I'll never forget the wannabe tarot reader who worked behind the counter at a local occult shop. She was itching to be one of the staff readers, but the shop owners were hesitant due to her limited experience. After a round of begging, they relented and put her on the schedule.

The first person who came for a reading with this beginner was a client who had worked with me previously. He enjoyed his reading so much that he wanted his daughter to get one too. It wasn't long before the reader botched that reading. She was so nervous that she stammered and rambled, and the man got mad. The shop was forced to refund his money, and she left in tears. This is what happens when you are not qualified. I've heard plenty of stories like this about other inexperienced readers over the years. Worse, some of them have done real damage that other readers like me have had to clean up.

Please give yourself time to get to know the cards. Don't rush into this profession. Take classes, read for as many people as you can, and develop your chops.

Author Mary K. Greer wrote an excellent piece on her blog titled *Suggestions for Becoming a Professional Tarot Reader* (*https://marykgreer.com/2009/11/12/sugges-tions-for-becoming-a-professional-tarot-reader/*). She recommends having a "rite of passage" where you "volunteer for a full day (or better yet, a weekend) at a charity or benefit event and donate everything to the cause."

Mary also adds: "The point is to read non-stop (except for necessary breaks), even to the point of exhaustion (drink plenty of water!). There's a point beyond which a part of you doesn't care what you say anymore, and you totally let go. You'll be surprised at what happens then and how accurate you become when you finally bypass your critic."

I think this is wise advice. In fact, I am a champion of people doing *many* of these events before going pro. This experience will separate the professionals from the hob-byists and help you build your skills fast.

Develop Your Plan

Once you've determined that you have mad skills, it's time to get going. Before you even begin setting up a business, you also need to reflect on what kind of business you want and the *people* you want to serve. Clarity will save you a lot of aggravation in the long run and may prevent costly mistakes. Meditate on what makes *you* happy. If you don't, you run the risk of hating this work or becoming burned out quickly.

Reflect on These Questions

1. Do you want to see clients in person? If so, will you want an office or will you meet your clients at a different location?

2. Will you offer readings by phone or email?

3. Do you wish to work parties or other public events such as a Renaissance Faire?

4. Will you wear costumes?

5. Do you like to work with a particular population? Are there some people for whom you may not feel comfortable reading?

6. Will you offer other services such as massage or aromatherapy?

7. Who is your ideal client? The more clarity you have on whom you want to serve, the more effective you'll be as a business person and the easier it will be for you to create marketing materials that get results.

8. With what situations are you good at dealing (for example, relationships)? For which situations are you *not* good at giving advice? Be clear on what services you offer as well as your expertise and, more importantly, what you don't offer (for example, as I have said a few times, I don't offer advice on gambling because this is something I do not believe in).

9. Are you going to invest in a website? (My advice—you should.) If so, are you going to do it yourself or hire a web designer?

10. What hobbies or activities make you the happiest? What gets you psyched?

When you are clear about your vision, you need to get down to the nitty-gritty.

Set Up the Foundation

Do not neglect setting up your business like a real business. In other words, choose a business structure and understand what it entails.

In the United States, most tarot readers work as a sole proprietorship. The IRS (*www.irs.gov/*) describes this type of business as follows:

A sole proprietor is someone who owns an unincorporated business by himself or herself.

While this is the simplest way to go and requires little to no paperwork in some cases, there are a few disadvantages to consider:

1. Raising capital for a sole proprietorship is more difficult because an unrelated investor has less peace of mind concerning the use and security of his or her investment and the investment is more difficult to formalize; other types of business entities have more documentation.

2. As a business becomes successful, the risks accompanying the business tend to grow. The primary disadvantage of a proprietorship is that the owner and all their personal assets are responsible for all of the liabilities of the business.

In other words, if your business gets sued for any reason, your personal assets are on the line.

Another route to go would be as a limited liability corporation, or LLC. The IRS describes this type of business as follows:

A Limited Liability Company (LLC) is a business structure allowed by state statute. LLCs are popular because, similar to a corporation, owners have limited personal liability for the debts and actions of the LLC. Other features of LLCs are more like a partnership, providing management flexibility and the benefit of pass-through taxation.

Setting up an LLC requires some paperwork and initially a fee to file the papers (this fee varies from state to state; it's usually around $200). Each year, your state may require you to file papers and pay a small fee (usually about $25).

While taking this route may seem tedious, it will protect you and your assets should the unlikely event come that someone decides to sue you.

Many cities or counties may require a license to do business. If you don't have one, your business may be considered illegal. The fees are usually small, and you can easily take care of them by visiting with your local county clerk, or you can simply have your lawyer handle it. Be sure to check out zoning compliance rules also to make sure the space you own or rent is zoned for your business. A special license also may be required if you are running your business out of your home. While these are all tedious details, setting yourself up as an LLC could perhaps save you a lot of drama down the road.

If you are going to use a business name other than your personal name (also known as a DBA, Doing Business As, or fictitious name), be sure to check with your state to make sure the name is not being used by someone else. You can find this through your state's website (such as *www.wisconsin.gov*). Contact or visit your local county clerk's office or your state government to register your DBA. Some states may require you to place a fictitious name notice in a local newspaper for a specific period of time. The costs for this are usually minimal.

If you live in a country other than the United States, laws and requirements may be different. You'll need to consult with your government to see what you must do to get legit.

Consider Insurance

While there are no special types of insurance for tarot readers in the US, you may want to consider getting a business owner's policy (BOP), especially if you set up your business as a sole proprietorship. This insurance will protect your assets in the unlikely event that someone decides to sue you.

Also, if you see clients in your home, you'll want to purchase additional home insurance (most insurance companies offer insurance for home offices). It is far more likely a client would sue you for falling at your office than for getting a bad reading. Protect yourself as much as you can. If you are doing readings only over the phone or via email, you may not need home office insurance.

If you are full-time self-employed, you may also need to purchase health insurance, disability or long-term care insurance, and life insurance (life insurance is vital if you have people who are dependent on your income).

Because of the high cost of health insurance, many tarot readers I know keep their day job for the benefits and choose to do tarot part-time on the side. If purchasing health insurance is too costly for you, this option may be something to consider.

Determine Starting Costs

You don't have to start out with a lot of money to begin your business. But you should make sure the basics are covered. Here is the bare minimum of what you will need to set aside money for (of course, you may not need all of these):

- Business setup fees (business license, etc.)

- Office space (unless you plan on using your home or a coffee shop)

- Phone (actual phone, phone line)

- Business cards and promotional materials (brochures, ads, etc.)

- An appointment book to schedule meetings with clients

- Website, which includes the domain, hosting, web designer, internet service provider, and email address

- Business support professionals, which may include an accountant, a lawyer, artists, a financial advisor

- Tarot cards (you'll want a couple of decks on hand in case they get ruined)

- A bookkeeping system

- Bank account solely for your business as well as a business credit card

- Notepads, pens, or tape recorder and tapes for clients

- Computer

- Insurance (health, liability)

- Advertising budget for email newsletters, Google ads, etc.

- Office equipment (desk, file cabinets, papers)

A good rule of thumb is to have six months' worth of income set aside if you plan on jumping in cold turkey. If you are planning to do this on the side until you have a regular list of clients, you may not need as much.

Set Rates

After you have decided it is time to set up shop, you need to figure out how much to charge for your services. This is a loaded topic for many reasons. The main issues are around what to charge and how to deal with the whole "this is a gift" thing.

Before I dive into what to charge, let's tackle that gift notion. There are some people, and some of them are fellow tarot readers, who preach that you should never charge for a tarot reading because it's a "gift." Therefore, you're expected to do it for free. Somehow that makes it noble, I guess. Frankly, I never understood that line of thinking.

While some people may be gifted tarot readers, it's a skill. *Period.* And any skilled labor deserves to be paid.

Also, there needs to be an equal exchange of energy; otherwise, people won't respect the wisdom delivered . . . or your time. Don't believe me? Try giving out free readings on social media. You'll not only get slammed with requests but also have to deal with abusive types who expect more, more, and more. Such exchanges will quickly zap your energy and goodwill.

When people pay for your services, they treat them with more respect. That's because they have skin in the game. They've invested with you. That being said, if you're not comfortable with charging and truly do view reading as a gift, have at it. As long as you have other means of support, if that makes you as happy as the Sun, be my guest.

As far as what to charge, you'll have to go with your gut. Some people recommend looking around to see what the going rate is, but I don't subscribe to that approach. Instead, figure out what you need to live comfortably and let that number dictate your price. For example, if you need to make $1,000 a week and can see only ten clients a week, your total may need to be at least $100 per reading.

When you're first starting out, you may choose to charge less. That's fine. As you build your skills and reputation, you can begin charging more. You may encounter the odd client who wants to talk about the "reader across town" who charges less. This may be a way of seeking a discount. I always reply: "It sounds like that reader is more aligned with your budget, so it might make more sense for you to continue to work with them."

I also want to remind you that when people are paying you, they are paying for your time. You cannot put a price tag on that.

Remember You Are Not Here to Fix People

Many people go into tarot as a profession because they want to help people. But sometimes that can lead to advice giving and trying to "fix" people. Keep in mind that you and tarot cannot do that. People have to want to change their lives and must be willing to do the work. You may be able to show them a path. You may be able to give an opinion. But you cannot fix their lives for them. Do not try to take on that responsibility.

Seeing a client in the same old position year after year can be frustrating. You may even wonder why the hell they are getting a tarot reading in the first place. Some people approach tarot like a magic wand: They don't want to do the work. They are hoping that the cards will somehow show a magic solution. These people are tough to read and can zap your morale. Try not to take it personally if they are unwilling to lift a finger to shift their lives. It is not your life to manage.

Handle Difficult Sitters

If you decide to read for the general public, you are going to encounter some aggravating types from time to time. You'll need to be prepared. Here are some of the various situations you'll need to stay alert for:

1. Skeptics. These are a type you'll run into more often than the other usual suspects. Their goal is to prove you wrong. If you don't mind working with these types, you might just surprise them. The key: you'll need to be confident. Even then, they might walk away, saying your reading was "bullshit." The truth is: they don't want to believe any of this can work.

2. People who say, "I don't want to say too much." Clients who lead with that statement are letting you know right off the bat that they want to test you. Like the skeptic, they want you to prove yourself. But unlike the skeptic, they might actually want a reading. Frankly, I find this mindset disrespectful. If you don't trust the reader, why are you there? It's like going to a doctor and saying, "I won't tell you my symptoms because I want you to magically tell me what's wrong."

3. Penny-pinchers. These clients are frustrating. They want to make sure they get their "money's worth," so they'll do everything to extend the reading. This may include trying to keep you on the phone when the session is over or sending

follow-up questions while feigning confusion. You'll need to be strict with your boundaries on this. When I used to offer email readings, I had one woman who always tried to keep the reading going. She'd contact me and say she was "so confused" as a way to get me to deliver more. One time she dared to say, "I understand you want to work smarter, not harder, but can you really give me enough information with three cards?" I fired her.

4. Pessimists. They are another type of challenging client. If they approach the reading like Eeyore, nothing you say will make a difference. These people don't need a tarot reading; they need help.

5. Those with inappropriate questions. Recently, a woman sat down at the table and said, "I have a question for you, and you're not going to like it. When am I going to die?" I told her that she was right—I didn't like the question, and I refused to answer it. If a question makes you uncomfortable, you can take a pass too.

6. Creeps and freaks. I've had male clients hit on me, touch themselves under the table, suggest a threesome with their wives, and threaten me when they didn't like the reading I gave their wives. I've also had people freak out in the office, step over my boundaries, show up unannounced at ten o'clock at night demanding I see them, arrive drunk, come in a disguise after they were fired—you get the picture. There are some real jerks out there and some scary types too. This is one of the main reasons why I no longer see people in person. If you are going to allow people into your space, you'll want to have some safety measures in place just in case that one-off person decides to go ballistic on you . . . or tries to corner you for a kiss on the way out the door. This stuff rarely happens, but you'll need to be ready.

7. The cursed. These clients are convinced that their problems are the result of a "curse." They want to believe their problems are caused by supernatural forces, not by bad choices. In some cases, they've been to another reader who has convinced them that this is the case (and the reader offers to "remove it" for a large sum of money!). They don't want to hear common sense; they want to believe that nothing is their fault. If someone isn't willing to take full responsibility for their life, a deck of tarot cards won't be much help.

8. The impaired. If clients show up drunk or stoned, send them away. They are not going to hear anything you say and will waste your time and energy. An impaired person is in no mind frame for a tarot reading. Signals get crossed and you will end up aggravated.

Now, those may be nightmare scenarios, but with a few solid boundaries, you can keep them to a minimum.

Create Policies

Whether you are a tarot pro or a newbie, you can take steps to ensure that you keep the crazy to a minimum in your tarot world. With clear policies and boundaries, you can prevent the wrong people from booking readings with you in the first place.

Take a moment to think about what kinds of boundaries are important to you. What readings might you refuse to do for a client? What are the consequences should someone step over your boundaries?

Consider what makes you feel safe and then draft a solid set of boundaries. Post them on your site so people know what you will or won't put up with in your biz.

Handle Delicate Situations

Other situations that might arise in your office require special handling. The person who is going through a major transition and is scared. The terminally ill client who is thinking about the end. The suicidal woman who needs support. These types of situations are not the norm, but they may come to your tarot table from time to time. Sometimes you may be the last line of hope.

To be a good tarot reader, you need to have a great deal of common sense but also empathy. Active listening is necessary, and a no-judgement zone is mandatory. Create a sacred space where your clients feel safe talking about what's on their mind. People should feel free talking about any and all situations with you. It goes without saying, but confidentiality is a must. What is said in your office stays in your office.

A few words of advice:

- Always be honest about what you see. You can find a way to be straight up and kind in your delivery.

- Don't play doctor or therapist. That means do not try diagnosing or prescribing treatment. You must never, ever, take that role, even if clients are seeking that kind of help from you. Set the tone immediately by letting them know that you are not a licensed physician or psychologist, and ethically you cannot diagnose, prescribe, or treat their situation. You must also refrain from playing lawyer or any other licensed professional. This is not your job . . . and could land you in trouble if your advice is wrong.

- Don't speak in absolutes. ("You're definitely going to get divorced." "You're totally going to live.") Here's something you may not want to hear: you could be wrong either way. You do not want to give false hope or add fear to an already emotionally tender situation.

- Don't be pitying or let your own fears about death, illness, loss, heartbreak, and so on get in the way of delivering a good reading. If you have anxiety about your clients' situation, that can lead to projection, which will taint the reading. A present, objective reader is what clients need. Keep your own feelings neutral. If you cannot do that, you may be better off refraining from the reading.

- Don't bring your own story into the mix. ("My cousin Serena had cancer, but now she's fine! You will be too!") Sharing your story is tempting, but although that may offer some insights, it also takes the energy away from your clients' situation. Keep the focus on your clients and their questions, not your family history.

- Don't bring your religious beliefs into the reading or restrict your clients from talking about theirs. Some clients may wish to discuss things such as the afterlife or their relationship to God, Spirit, Buddha, goddesses, or angels. Or they may well be atheists who don't believe in any of that. Whatever the case, their beliefs should be treated with the utmost respect.

- Do create a safe space where clients can express their feelings freely. Your tarot office should be a sacred container where clients can share their fears and emotions openly. Be compassionate and allow them to vent, cry, or unload their frustrations without judgement.

- Do allow your clients to touch your hand during the reading or hug you if they need to. I have found that a simple hand on the shoulder can be helpful, especially if the mood gets emotional. (Believe it or not, some of my clients have requested that my cats sit in on their reading. A pet on the lap can be soothing when discussing fearful subjects.)

- Do encourage your clients to steer away from "Yes/No" questions. You do not want to be in a position where you are making decisions for them.

- Do encourage your clients to ask expansive questions that point to a particular theme, path, or life lesson. (For example, "How can I use this difficult experience to heal old wounds with my family?" Or "What should I be focusing on right now to stay as positive as possible?") This approach can take the reading from good to deep and purposeful.

- Do something to clear your energy after the reading so that you're not carrying around any sadness, anger, or fear that could potentially impact your ability to serve your next round of clients.

When a Tarot Client Is Suicidal

First of all, if clients disclose that they want to end their lives during a tarot reading, *always* take that threat seriously. Do not brush off such statements or assume that tossing a few cards will change their mind.

Keep in mind that you may be the first person they've told. Sometimes people will open up during a tarot session and reveal things that they may not tell their loved ones. Give them a safe space to talk about their feelings. *Listen* with empathy. Sometimes this can make all the difference. If they don't want to talk, do not force them. Instead, touching their hand or shoulder or even verbal support can help.

Next, you need to encourage these clients to seek support from the proper resources. While a tarot reading can offer guidance, it isn't the solution, and it's *never* a substitute for professional mental help. Unless you are a licensed therapist, you cannot take on that role.

Have a list of referrals on hand. Here are a few:

- **Crisis Text Line:** *crisistextline.org*

  Send a text anytime, 24/7, and a trained counselor will listen to you and reply. Totally free. Text and get support if you're struggling with anxiety, depression, suicidal thoughts, or any type of emotional crisis.

- **Suicide Prevention Lifeline:** *suicidepreventionlifeline.org* or 1.800.273.8255

  Call and get help anytime, 24/7, and a volunteer will listen and help you settle your nervous system and bring you back to a calmer place where you can think clearly.

- **TalkSpace:** *https://talkspace.com/*

  Text and chat with a licensed therapist. Professional therapy that's affordable and convenient. You don't have to get dressed, drive across town, and find parking. A real therapist . . . right on your phone!

- **7Cups:** *www.7cups.com*

  The world's most extensive emotional support system. Connect to caring listeners for free emotional support. They also can connect you to licensed therapists.

In some cases, you'll need to be ready to intervene. If you know their loved ones, reach out. Let them know what's going on. Yes, you will be breaking client confidentiality, but you may save a life. If you don't know anyone who may be connected to them, err on the side of caution and reach out to a professional.

Keep in mind that not everyone will disclose their situation to you. Some people may be keeping these thoughts to themselves. Or they may make the decision to end their lives impulsively. It's too easy to blame yourself for "not seeing it in the cards," but you cannot take on that responsibility. No one can see it all, despite their best efforts.

Clients may reach out to you in desperation. If they do and you can get them in, please do. Sometimes just having someone to talk to may help. But if you cannot squeeze them in and you feel the client might do something rash, once again, refer them to the proper help and be ready to contact their family if you know them.

Working with a client who is going through a crisis can also be hard on you. Make sure that you are practicing extreme self-care in these types of situations.

If a client does decide to end their life, you may feel awful. You might grieve or beat yourself up. If you're feeling sad, make sure that you get support too. When people commit suicide, the effects are devastating not just for the family members who are left behind, but also for the service providers and other folks who tried to help.

When Someone Freaks Out

I've had a few occasions in which a client had a meltdown in my office. Usually, this reaction had nothing to do with the reading. The client was at a breaking point and needed a place to unload. In one situation, a woman suddenly stood up, crying and talking about voices that were commanding her to do things. (In that case, I contacted her mother immediately after she left, and she was able to get into a facility.)

Sometimes, though, a reading can trigger a reaction. One such situation happened at a tarot party. I was working in a gorgeous ballroom for a group of doctors. One of the wives sat down at the table. The cards showed an argument with a man about children. Suddenly, she bolted upright and screamed at the top of her lungs, "You're full of shit!"

I was in shock, and so were the other party-goers. A woman standing near me touched my shoulder and whispered, "You're actually right. She wants to adopt a child, and her husband won't let her."

What do you do when this happens?

First of all, you must remain calm. You might be scared or want to cry (I sure wanted to cry at that party). Gather yourself as best as you can. Allow the client to vent if they need to. Speak in a neutral, reassuring tone. This way of responding will often help you get control of the situation. Refer the client to someone who can help them and end the reading as gently as possible.

The most important thing is to calm them down . . . and move them out of your presence.

In the case of a party like the one I mentioned, you have the luxury of other people around to support the aggravated client . . . and you. Excuse yourself, go to the bathroom, splash a bit of water on your face, wash your hands, take deep breaths, and go back out there. If the situation persists or escalates, you may need to leave. I've never had to do that, but it is always a possibility.

When You Need to Fire Someone

In some situations, a client will not be the right fit for you. If you have an intake form as I do, you can quickly assess whether this is the situation. In that case, you can simply refund their money and let them know that you're not their reader.

Let's say, however, that you don't have an intake form. Or you do but the person seems okay on paper and then proves that they are anything but an ideal client in person.

You must remember this: you deserve to be comfortable with the people you serve as much as you want them to feel the same with you. If they cannot treat you with respect and want to trample over your boundaries, they need to go.

The easiest way to fire someone is via email. That way, there is no room for negotiation, and the abuse is minimized. Be aware that when you fire a client, they may go out of their way to slam you to other people or leave bad reviews online. They are hurt and angry . . . and unwilling to take responsibility for their role in getting dismissed. It sucks when this happens, but every business owner will encounter it at some point.

The customer is not always right, and you don't have to take abuse from anyone, ever.

Establish the Reading Process

When a client comes to work with me, this is my routine.

I begin with an introduction. If they have worked with me before, there is no need to tell them about myself. But if they are new to me, I want them to know what I'm all about. An introduction doesn't need to be lengthy. It might be a greeting, introducing yourself, and showing them to the tarot table if it's an in-person session. If you're reading over the phone, a quick "Hello, how are you?" should suffice.

The first thing I do is pull an oracle card. I start out with this as a way to relax the client, break the ice, and get their mind ready for tarot. Sometimes people come to me straight from work or some other event, and they may be harried. Taking a moment to relax while I read the oracle card calms their nerves. You might want to try this approach too. Or you may have another method, such as an opening prayer or invocation. Just find something to create a relaxing vibe.

Next, I explain what we are going to do. That step includes sharing the spreads we'll use, how many questions we will have time for, and my process.

I recommend recording your sessions for clients. For one, this is an excellent way for them to reflect back on the meeting. Also, sometimes people hear only what they want to hear. Having a recording allows them to check in to what is actually said.

If you're seeing a client in-person, give them the cards and tell them how to shuffle and cut the cards. If you're working over the phone, begin shuffling. Ask the client to take a few slow, deep breaths and to say "stop" when they want you to stop.

Lay out the cards and begin the reading. I always start out with a general outlook, but in some cases, we go straight to questions.

Give the client time to ask questions about the spread or about any pertinent issues. Also, let them know when the session is almost up. I announce it by saying we have time for one more question. Sometimes the client will respond, "Oh no, I have three more." I will then tell them that they can choose one, or I'm only pulling a card for each question. I never allow the reading to go over the allotted time, and neither should you get in the habit; otherwise, people will expect this every time.

Finally, I do a closing spread to pull it all together. You may want to do this or offer another type of oracle card to seal the deal.

Bid the client farewell and cleanse your deck. My friend Briana Saussy recommends washing your hands between each appointment. This is a genius way to cleanse the energy!

This routine works well and gives the clients a comprehensive, professional tarot experience.

A Few Tips as You Begin Growing Your Business

1. Get some business cards, and always keep a few with you. Even in this day and age of Google, business cards are a great way to promote your work. I cannot tell you the number of times people have said to me that they found the card in an old purse and remembered that they hadn't had a reading with me in a while! Plus, you never know when you'll run into someone who wants a reading!

2. Do *not* barter for your services. Although you may be tempted to do so, you will quickly end up with a lot of stuff you don't want. Massage therapists are notorious for trying to swap with me. I'm picky about who touches me, so it's no dice. If you're going to trade for a service or product, make sure it's something you really want and is equal in value to your services.

3. An online scheduler will save you the hassle of setting up appointments and nagging people. You can send clients a link to your online scheduler or have it right on your site. This tool eliminates back and forth too, which can waste hours of your time.

4. Use social media and other sources (such as ads in local papers) to promote your work. Marketing is essential if you want to build a name.

5. Offer to speak or read at community events such as farmers markets and spirit fairs. This is a fast way to grow a local audience.

6. Attend tarot conferences. This is another way to get your face out there and to meet your peers. There is nothing better than the support of fellow tarot pros!

7. Encourage people to refer others to you. You may want to have a referral program when you first start out. For example, "refer ten people, and your next reading is free." *But* don't keep that going too long. I have found that sometimes such programs lead to people sending any old person to you just to get that freebie. Plus, you'll have to keep track, and that can be a pain as your business grows.

8. While costumes can be fun, I refrain from those. I think it makes people treat the work as a joke. You're more likely to get folks who respect your work if you ditch the typical fortune-teller costume and wear your regular duds. That being said, if you enjoy dressing like Morticia Adams, go for it! Some people want the goth experience and expect a reader to dress the part.

9. Keep a regular schedule of hours. Do not work outside those hours. Sometimes people will request an emergency reading. If you feel the situation warrants it, go ahead and do the reading. I do not offer that service because I have found it leads to more emergency readings, usually on the same subject.

10. Parties are an excellent way to grow your business. I've gotten tons of referrals from the days when I did bachelorette parties! One time, I was hired, and so was a male stripper. There I was, tossing cards while a greased-up, deeply tanned man with a mullet and neon green G-string gyrated around the room. It was . . . interesting.

11. Self-care needs to be a priority. You can quickly burn out from this work. Know when to take time off and do it. You don't need to be on 24/7, and you shouldn't.

A tarot business can be a satisfying way to earn a living while serving others. After all, who doesn't want to help people? If your heart is in the right place, this may become your life's calling too.

Alrighty—that's the skinny on the tarot business.

• • •

I'd like to remind you one more time to be mindful of the impact you may have on people's lives. Choose your words with care. Be compassionate. Try not to judge. Above all, let your readings be full of hope. Because life always is, no matter what. Let people walk away feeling empowered and ready to live their best life. Do that and you'll inspire folks to rise up and live conscious, healthy lives.

And that's all I've got for you, friends.

In conclusion: Tarot rocks and intuition is Queen!

I hope that this book has given you a thorough intro to intuitive tarot reading and how my tarot brain operates. For some, my wish is that it inspired you to take it seriously and read professionally.

I'd like to finish by saying that tarot is always evolving, and there are new decks, insights, and ways to use the tarot coming out all the time. You mustn't get too stuck in your ways or develop what I call "bad tarot habits" of only seeing the cards from one perspective, including mine.

Keep an open mind. Take classes when you can. Attend conferences. Read as many books as you can get your hands on, including the classics such as *78 Degrees of Wisdom* by Rachel Pollack and *Tarot for Yourself* by Mary K. Greer. Get readings from other tarot pros and see how they approach the cards. Test-drive new decks and spreads. Never assume that you'll be a "master" of this. (Tarot has a way of mastering you!)

No matter how long you're at it, remain curious. That way, your tarot practice will continue to evolve as you do.

Keep shuffling,

—Theresa

Recommended Reading

Seventy-Eight Degrees of Wisdom by Rachel Pollack

Tarot Wisdom by Rachel Pollack

The New Tarot Handbook: Master the Meanings of the Cards by Rachel Pollack

21 Ways to Read a Tarot Card by Mary K. Greer

Understanding the Tarot Court by Mary K. Greer and Thomas Little

Tarot for Your Self by Mary K. Greer

Who Are You in the Tarot? by Mary K. Greer

The Complete Book of Tarot Reversals by Mary K. Greer

Kitchen Table Tarot by Melissa Cynova

Modern Tarot by Michelle Tea

The Tarot Coloring Book by Theresa Reed (that's me!)

Tarot for Troubled Times by Shaheen Miro and Theresa Reed

Learning the Tarot by Joan Bunning

Tarot Spreads: Layouts and Techniques to Empower Your Readings by Barbara Moore

The Secret Language of Tarot by Wald Amberstone and Ruth Ann Amberstone

Acknowledgments

Thank you to my Weiser family for taking a chance on me. I am so happy to be with you!

Gratitude to Kathryn Sky-Peck for believing in me. I appreciate you so much!

Grazie to Chuck Hutchinson for polishing this book up to perfection!

Major thanks to Megan Lang, the sharpest grammarian I know.

Hugs to my writing mentor, Alexandra Franzen, who always helps me find my words.

Gratitude to Rachel Pollack and Mary K. Greer, who paved the way and blazed the trails.

Tons of love to Briana Saussy, Shaheen Miro, Simone Salmon, Andrew McGregor, Carrie Paris, Joanna Powell Colbert, Hilary Parry Haggerty, Al Juarez, Pleasant Gehman, Gabriela Herstik, Angela Mary Magick, Danielle Cohen, Ruth Ann Amberstone, Wald Amberstone, Connie Kick, Melissa Cynova, Benebell Wen, Jenna Matlin, Chris-Anne Donnelly, Jamie Sawyer, Jaymi Elford, Arwen Lynch Poe, Tammi Kapitanski, Seth Vermilyea, Mantis, Tanya Geisler, Elliot Eernisse, Mary Ellen Pride, Suzi Dronzek, Heatherleigh Navarre, Naha Armády, Diane Bloom, Chris Zydel, Fabeku Fatunmise, Jessica Schumacher, Georgianna Boehnke, Donnaleigh de la Rose, Peggie Reinke, Jackie Dayen, Guy Dayen, Damien Echols, Lorri Davis, and so many other folks who have given me lots of love and support over the years—you know who you are.

Gratitude to my tarot clients, some of whom have been with me since the beginning. It's been my honor to serve you.

Thanks to my tarot and yoga students; I've learned so much from *you*.

Much love to my children, Megan and Nick.

Deepest love and thanks to my ever-patient Virgo husband, Terry, for keeping the house clean and my sanity intact while I wrote two books in a year (again).

Lastly, my appreciation for my mother, who taught me to trust my gut, no matter what. I wish you were here to see all the books I'm creating. I miss you.

About the Author

THERESA REED is a tarot veteran who's been doing tarot professionally for over thirty years. She's the author of *The Tarot Coloring Book, Astrology for Real Life,* and the coauthor of *Tarot for Troubled Times.* In addition to reading the cards, she loves teaching and runs several classes on tarot and astrology. Her philosophy is: "The cards tell a story, but you write the ending." She loves yoga, whipping up feasts in her kitchen, cats, hip-hop, and her husband and children. You can find her at *www.thetarotlady.com.*

To Our Readers

Weiser Books, an imprint of Red Wheel/Weiser, publishes books across the entire spectrum of occult, esoteric, speculative, and New Age subjects. Our mission is to publish quality books that will make a difference in people's lives without advocating any one particular path or field of study. We value the integrity, originality, and depth of knowledge of our authors.

Our readers are our most important resource, and we appreciate your input, suggestions, and ideas about what you would like to see published.

Visit our website at *www.redwheelweiser.com* to learn about our upcoming books and free downloads, and be sure to go to *www.redwheelweiser.com/newsletter* to sign up for newsletters and exclusive offers.

You can also contact us at *info@rwwbooks.com* or at

Red Wheel/Weiser, LLC
65 Parker Street, Suite 7
Newburyport, MA 01950